# HELPING CHILDREN TO LEARN THROUGH A MOVEMENT PERSPECTIVE

**MOLLIE DAVIES**

SERIES EDITOR TINA BRUCE

Paul Chapman
Publishing

Reprinted 2001

Paul Chapman Publishing Ltd
A SAGE Publications Company
6 Bonhill Street
London  EC2A 4PU

SAGE Publications Inc
2455 Teller Road
Thousand Oaks, California 91320

SAGE Publications India Pvt Ltd
32, M-Block Market
Greater Kailash - I
New Delhi  110 048

British Library Cataloguing in Publication data
A catalogue record for this book  is available from the British Library

ISBN    0 7619 7295 1

Library of Congress catalog card number

Reprinted for SAGE publications by Alden Press

First published 1995

Impression number 10 9 8 7 6 5 4 3 2 1
Year                    1999 1998 1997 1996 1995

This book is dedicated to Molly Brearley CBE, Principal of the Froebel Institute College from 1955–1970, and Chris Athey, M.Ed, formerly Principal Lecturer in Education and Leverhulme Research Fellow at the Froebel College. Each in her own way has helped me towards an understanding of the rich variety of ways in which young children learn, and both have generously supported my attempts to identify movement as a crucial factor in that process.

# ACKNOWLEDGEMENTS

These go a long way back to my early teaching days and continue through time to my years at the Froebel College and later at the Roehampton Institute. To all my colleagues, at various stages of my teaching career, I am grateful for the many years of sharing which took place and for the wide range of opportunities given to me, many of which have provided material for my writing.

More specifically, but also un-named, are the parents and teachers who, sometimes with no prior notice, allowed me to photograph their children and to record their activities and conversations. Their interest, curiosity, and generosity were an important source of encouragement to me. I hope that when they read what has been written they will understand what a significant contribution they have made.

Thanks go to friends who became photographers, and photographers who became friends, and especially to Terry Kane and Rob De Wet who worked with so much understanding and patience in my quest for meaningful illustrations. I would also like to thank Dee De Wet and her junior class for allowing me to use illustrative material from their dance project. Photographic credits are as follows: Chris Davies: figure 3; Jean Jarrell: figure 22; Michael Kane: figures 25 and 45; Terry Kane: figures 6 and 55; Rob De Wet: figures 8, 9, 15, 28, 40, 47 and 67; the Academy of Indian Dance: figure 73; and finally figures 41, 42, 43, 48 and 65, © Catherine Ashmore, have been reproduced from *Childsplay* by Lucy Jackson (Thorsons, 1993) with the kind permission of the photographer, Catherine Ashmore, and the publishers.

I am particularly grateful to Chris Athey for her detailed reading of the manuscript, and for her humorous way of providing constructive criticism. Thanks go also to Mary Wilkinson for the careful attention she gave to the presentation of the movement classification and its use in expressive behaviour, and to Jean Jarrell for her meticulous proof reading and the provision of diagrams in Chapter 1.

Finally, I wish to convey my thanks to Tina Bruce who has given me such support during the writing of this book. She has entered wholeheartedly into every phase of its production and I am most grateful to her for her encouragement, gentle guidance – and for keeping faith.

# CONTENTS

# SERIES PREFACE – 0–8 YEARS

At most times in history and in most parts of the world, the first eight years of life have been seen as the first phase of living. Ideally, during this period, children learn who they are; about those who are significant to them; and how their world is. They learn to take part, and how to contribute creatively, imaginatively, sensitively and reflectively.

Children learn through and with the people they love and the people who care for them. They learn through being physically active, through real, direct experiences, and through learning how to make and use symbolic systems, such as play, language and representation. Whether children are at home, in nursery schools, classes, family centres, day nurseries, or playgroups, workplace nurseries, primary schools or whatever, they need informed adults who can help them. The series will help those who work with young children, in whatever capacity, to be as informed as possible about this first phase of living.

From the age of eight years all the developing and learning can be consolidated, hopefully in ways which build on what has gone before.

In this series, different books emphasise different aspects of the first phase of living. *Getting to Know You* and *Learning to be Strong* give high status to adults (parents and early-childhood specialists of all kinds) who love and work with children. *Getting to Know You*, by Lynne Bartholomew and Tina Bruce focuses on the importance of adults in the lives of children. Observing children in spontaneous situations at Redford House Nursery (a workplace nursery) and in a variety of other settings, the book emulates the spirit of Susan Isaacs. This means using theory to interpret observations and recording the progress of children as they are supported and extended in their development and learning. The book is full of examples of good practice in record-keeping. Unless we know and understand our children, unless we act effectively on what we know, we cannot help them very much.

*Learning to be Strong*, by Margy Whalley, helps us to see how important it is that all the adults living or working with children act as a team. This is undoubtedly one of the most important kinds of partnership that human beings ever make. When adults come together and use their energy in an orchestrated way on behalf of the child, then quality and excellent progress are seen. Pen Green Centre for Under-fives and Families is the story of the development of a kind of partnership which Margaret McMillan would have admired. Beacons of excellence continue to shine and illuminate practice through the ages, transcending the passing of time.

Just as the first two books emphasise the importance of the adult helping the child, the next two focus *on* the child. John Matthews helps us to focus on one of the ways in which children learn to use symbolic systems. In *Helping Children to Draw and Paint in Early Childhood,* he looks at how children keep hold of the experiences they have through the process of representation. Children's drawings and paintings are looked at in a way which goes beyond the superficial, and help us to understand details. This means the adult can help the child better. Doing this is a complex process, but the book suggests ways which are easy to understand and is full of real examples.

In *Helping Children to Learn Through a Movement Perspective,* Mollie Davies, an internationally respected movement expert, with years of practical experience of working with young children, writes about the central place of movement within the learning process. In a lively, well-illustrated book, with lots of real examples, she makes a case for movement as a common denominator of the total development of children, and in this draws our attention to its integrating function. In addition to linking movement with physical development and movement with thinking she helps us to see how children's expressive and social behaviour can also be looked at through 'movement eyes'. She suggests ways in which its role can be highlighted in a variety of learning and teaching settings with a whole chaper devoted to dance – the art form of movement. The provision of a readily accessible movement framework gives excellent opportunities for adults to plan, observe, and record their children's development in movement terms.

Other books in the series will underline the importance of adults working together to become informed in order to help children develop and learn.

Clinging to dogma, 'I believe children need . . .' or saying 'What was good enough for me . . .' is not good enough. Children deserve better than that. The pursuit of excellence means being informed. This series will help adults increase their knowledge and understanding of the 'first phase of living', and to act in the light of this for the good of children.

TINA BRUCE

# INTRODUCTION

This book is about the multi-faceted role that movement plays in the lives of young children. It explores the nature and function of movement as a central part of their action, thinking and feeling, and highlights the pleasure and sense of well-being which is experienced as they are helped to realise their bodily potential. It advocates that attention given by adults to the development of their children's movement, and its significance in the learning process, is crucial right from the start of life. This is not only because it helps towards producing a well-tuned and articulate body, which in itself is a matter of considerable importance, but also because of the very real role movement plays in the development of feeling and thought.

Having observed ways in which children can be helped to develop thinking, expressing and socialising skills through movement, their roles as early performers, creators and spectators are looked at within dance – the art form of movement.

Photographic illustrations inform the text throughout. In places they 'become' the text. The purpose of these, along with the movement classification, contextual examples, and general guidelines in which they are embedded, is to spark off procedures and practices – or ways and means – which seem most appropriate to a particular setting. Any more specific use must be decided upon by the adults concerned, for not only are children unique but so also are the people who care, nurture and educate them.

# 1 WHAT IS MOVEMENT?

## EXAMINING THE THEORETICAL FRAMEWORK

Movement is so much a fundamental part of our everyday lives that, understandably, those concerned with child care and education may not necessarily see the need to classify what must, after all, seem obvious. The indivisibility of movement from human functioning may be one of the reasons why its importance in terms of child development is not always given the serious recognition it deserves. It is so indivisible, so implicit, that it 'goes without saying' and, therefore, sometimes eludes its rightful place within a study context.

As soon as children show the first signs of early reading skills, help is at hand. Resources, methods and procedures are actively sought and discussion within family units and between family units abounds. Similarly, as children's interests in numeracy become apparent, parents are the first to join in the bigger/smaller, taller/shorter phase of discrimination. Even if parents do not possess detailed information in these areas, realising its importance they seek it out and certainly provide toys and experiences which assist learning at this stage. In movement, too, important achievements are noted, valued and discussed with pride. Photograph albums are filled with pictures and captions documenting such events as early, unsteady steps, digging in the sand, kicking a ball and swimming without water wings.

In some instances adults 'sense' what knowledge is needed to help children consolidate or progress in their movement activities. But, however valuable and successful (or otherwise) this sensing may prove to be on specific occasions, it is unrelated to a much larger canvas of knowledge. The adults concerned need to extend beyond 'sensing' or 'gut reaction' for as Bruce (1987, p. 3) comments 'Gut reactions are difficult to articulate, yet articulation is essential if communication is considered a high priority'. If parents, carers, nursery nurses and teachers are to take responsibility for movement as an important area of children's experience they need to know what 'constitutes' movement just as they need to know about all the other areas of learning for which they make provision. The purpose of this chapter, therefore, is to provide a theoretical framework which will serve as a reference point, or identity kit, for the many examples of children's activities which illustrate subsequent chapters. It is also intended to provide a means of promoting, supporting, enriching and recording children's movement for all those concerned with the education of young children.

**THE BODY**
Action
Articulation
Design
Fluency
Shape

**DYNAMICS**
Weight
Space (qualitative)
Time
Flow

**SPACE**
Size
Extension
Zone
Level
Direction

**RELATIONSHIPS**
Between parts of
    the body
With objects
With people

*Figure 1    A general classification of movement in relation to young children from birth to eight years*

# THE BODY: WHAT TAKES PLACE

## Body Action

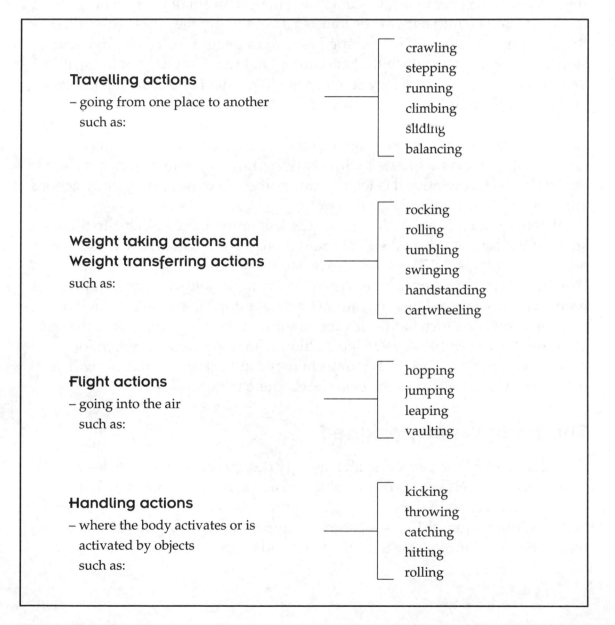

**Travelling actions**
– going from one place to another
  such as:

crawling
stepping
running
climbing
sliding
balancing

**Weight taking actions and
Weight transferring actions**
such as:

rocking
rolling
tumbling
swinging
handstanding
cartwheeling

**Flight actions**
– going into the air
  such as:

hopping
jumping
leaping
vaulting

**Handling actions**
– where the body activates or is
  activated by objects
  such as:

kicking
throwing
catching
hitting
rolling

*Figure 2   The body in action*

The body moving into action is a vital part of all movement activity whether it arises spontaneously or occurs in response to structured situations at home, in the play centre or at school. It is through the dynamic and spatial use of a growing number of separate and related actions, that children become increasingly competent and versatile in a variety of movement situations.

Travelling actions typify the play of very young children. As soon as they become independently mobile they invest all their actions in the space which they inhabit. At other times they enjoy staying put in small pockets of space and explore actions which support or transfer their weight; they rock, they roll over, they turn upside down. Overcoming gravity is a delight for all children and is something which remains with them throughout the first phase of living (0–8 years) and beyond. Before they can manage to push off and make themselves air-borne they jump from a stair or kerbstone which, in reality, means 'dropping down' rather than 'jumping down'. Being helped to jump by willing adults is a way of 'feeling what it is like' – an experience important to the development of any activity. Actions associated with dexterity, ranging from grip and release to sophisticated throwing and catching, are another set of important body actions children gradually add to their repertoire.

Parents and early childhood educators will immediately be able to think of some of the actions which their children can perform, particularly those which are current favourites. They will also be able to recall ways in which some of these have developed over time. When, for example, a turn became a spin, when a jump came out of a run, and when that jump lasted long enough to make a shape, or a turn in the air such as the one shown opposite and the one attempted by Lucy on page 92. Body action is an important ingredient of movement, particularly so for young children, and examples of these will be discussed in a variety of contexts in the chapters which follow.

## The body is well designed

The general public is becoming increasingly design conscious with designer products and labels now firmly established as indicators of prestige. In the professional worlds of dance and sport, design characteristics of the human body feature frequently. This is especially apparent in photographic images in the sports and dance sections of the press, and in specialist journals.

*Figure 3    Turning in the air: two actions in one*

## Symmetry and Asymmetry

Through its natural structure and the number and arrangement of limbs, the body of a baby is initially predominantly symmetric. However, at a very early stage habitual ways of moving, with emphasis on one side of the body over the other, frequently involve the use of asymmetry. Apart from the early reflex shaking and beating activities of very young babies, symmetry, brought about through equal emphasis of both sides of the body, is usually associated with evenness involving movement characterised by control and balance. Swinging, exerting two-sided movement of arms and legs, a low squat position near the ground frequently adopted by young children, or engagement in a hand spring enjoyed by eight-year-olds are common examples.

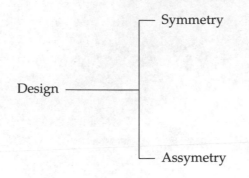

*Figure 4    The body is well designed*

Conversely, asymmetric movement is recognised by the way one side of the body is emphasised more than the other and where there is a lack of equivalence between the two sides. In contrast to the even balance associated with symmetric movement, asymmetry is characterised by off balance and less restrained movement which has a tendency to be on-going. Specific movement activities, such as early throwing behaviour, demand an appropriateness of body design but, apart from these, both children and adults usually have a natural preference for either two-sided or one-sidedness. A quick look around a group of children as they listen to a story, eat a meal, or engage in dramatic play will give clear indications of their preferences.

## Articulation

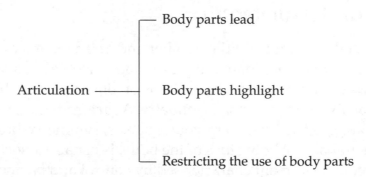

*Figure 5    The body is well articulated*

The well articulated body can emphasise the use of one part or several parts of the body. These may lead the movement as the head does when 'being a plane', or where hands go first to meet the ground on the way to a handstand. Parts of the body may be given a role of importance and highlighted as in the way the hands wave or the feet tap dance. Highlighting the varied use of body parts is natural for children at early stages of learning and an important experience for both skilled and inventive performance. So too, is the restricting of body parts, a limitation which children often impose upon themselves. 'No hands' is a special favourite and is illustrated for us here by Charlotte, aged seven, as she enjoys the see-saw.

*Figure 6    Self-imposed bodily restriction: no hands*

## Body Shapes

### Long and stretched
Body shape refers to the form of the body when a position is held and there are four of these which can be easily identified in children's movement play. The first is long and stretched and emphasises the use of one direction only. It stresses the dimension of length and in this shape body parts are aligned to

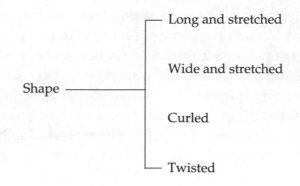

Shape
— Long and stretched
— Wide and stretched
— Curled
— Twisted

*Figure 7     The body can make a variety of shapes*

produce the effect of elongation and narrowness. This shape is seen clearly as children tunnel their way through hollow tubes, jump from a height, attempt a netball or basketball shot, play at parachuting, or are directed to 'stand up straight!' In figure 8, Eleanor, aged two-and-a-half, is responding to a suggestion to stretch up as tall as she can. As she does so her body becomes narrow and long as she pierces the space in an upward direction.

*Figure 8     An elongated body shape*

## Wide and stretched

The second body shape is also stretched but this time in terms of width. The natural tendency of two-dimensional movement results in this shape as arms and legs are stretched sideways into space, spreading away from the centre of the body and creating a tension between the limbs themselves. Children enjoy making two-dimensional star shapes early on as shown in figure 9 by Lucy and her mother. At around three or four they often use them to suggest 'being big', or as a barrier to stop someone, or something, getting past.

*Figure 9    Wide and stretched: a two-dimensional body shape*

Jumping in a star shape soon becomes a firm favourite and is often to be seen as children take off from walls, trees and apparatus or into the swimming pool. In swimming breast stroke, the star shape with its two-dimensionality of movement is emphasised as a child's body travels through the water, while spinning in a horizontal star shape may occur in a catherine wheel or spinning-top dance. The more complex activity of a cartwheel shows a moving, star-shaped image as the weight of the body is taken successively from hand to hand to foot to foot as the body revolves.

### Rounded

A third body shape, this time three-dimensional in character and which is essentially rounded, is often seen in rolling activities where the spine curves and the extremities meet – or almost meet – each other. The curve may sometimes be taken in the opposite direction, with the back of the head and the heels sharing the arc. This is a shape which constitutes part of athletic or acrobatic activity such as a backward dive or a pole vault. In expressive terms it is one often used by both contemporary and classical dancers.

### Twisted

The last of the four body shapes is twisted as different areas of the body pull against each other around one or more axes. A great favourite with young children, it is much used in dance and dramatic play associated with aspects of the natural environment such as gnarled trees, with witches, sea monsters and other imaginary creatures. The sinuous way in which young bodies twist and turn in and out of railings, small spaces and almost impossible gaps also show this particular body shape.

## Successive and simultaneous movements

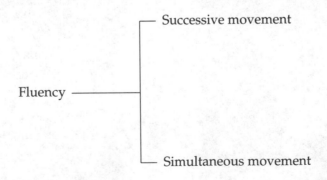

*Figure 10    The body has a natural fluency*

In successive movement, body parts are brought into play one after another in a wave-like, rippling action. Such movement has a fluidity about it and makes for continuity. It can be identified in the movement of young children as they grasp a low hanging branch and, starting with their feet, take their body through with the use of knees, hips, spine and head as they achieve balance the other side. Simultaneous movement, on the other hand, occurs when some, and at times all parts of the body, move at the same time. The 'togetherness', implicit in simultaneous movement, is present throughout the whole action, from the moment it starts until the end of its passage. An obvious example of this is when young children, in the style of premier league goalkeepers, hurl their bodies to protect the area of play under threat.

# DYNAMICS: HOW MOVEMENT TAKES PLACE

All human activity is to some extent dynamically and rhythmically charged and structured. Young children, like people at all stages of life, are recognised by the dynamic and rhythmic make-up which characterises their style of moving. It is the extent to which the factors of weight, qualitative space, time and flow are used and combined with each other which determines the rhythmic and dynamic differences between individual children and characterises 'how' they move. At times specific actions call for a particular rhythmic and dynamic mix in order for the response to be effective; the strong leg action in kicking a ball, the careful, slow threading of shoe laces, the vigorous shaking of a rattle or a

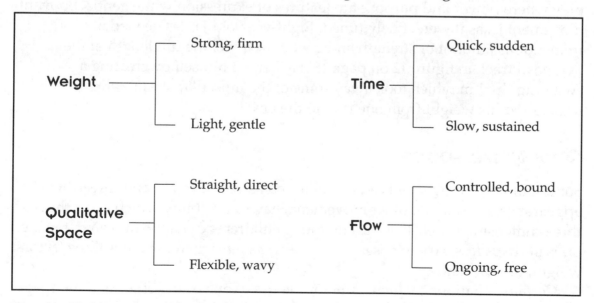

*Figure 11   The body moves dynamically and rhythmically*

tambourine. All these activities – kicking, threading and shaking – demand specific dynamic responses which have to be selected from the children's current repertoire. Obviously, making appropriate responses to specific daily challenges implies a rich dynamic range from which to select, a range which needs stimulating, supporting and enriching throughout the primary years. Ways in which these factors particularly relate to the expressive life of young children are looked at in greater detail in Chapter 6.

## Weight

Very young children, at about two years, understand the weight content of movement mainly in terms of opposites, of movement being either strong or light. As understanding increases so the finer discriminations of strength and force can be produced at will, as can degrees of gentleness at the other end of the continuum. Changes in the muscular tension of the body, which result in changes of energy and force, occur, for example, when children pit their energy against external structures. In order to pull up on the sides of a cot, onto a branch of a tree, or climb a rope, a strong grip of the hands, and strength in the shoulder girdle and arms, are needed to lift the body in defiance of its own weight. Strength and energy are required to jump far, high and wide, to kick a ball hard, and effectively hammer a nail into a piece of wood. A delicate touch is needed to make light brush marks on the paper, to stroke the hamster, or to catch a soap bubble on an outstretched hand. Firmness in dance is brought into play where power and purpose are features of expression while gentle, buoyant movement is, as it were, finely tuned. Eight-year-old James needed a tremendous amount of strength and energy to travel the full length of the overhead track in figure 12 on page 13. He helped himself by creating a swinging rhythm which took away some of the muscular strain as he transferred his weight from one ring to the next.

## Qualitative space

Some children's movement can be described as very straight and thread-like in appearance. In contrast, other movements have a flexibility which gives them a three-dimensional feel. This part of young children's dynamic movement make-up is perhaps less easy to observe in the early stages than the other three factors: weight, time and flow.

Certain situations call generally for the use of one or the other of these space elements. For example, children may use flexibility in putting their arms into

*Figure 12    Strength and energy are needed here*

the sleeves of their coat, twisting in and out of the banisters, or casting a magical spell. Directness is expressed in throwing activities for instance, and making contact between beater and drum. On other occasions, where the call for a particular space quality is less prescribed, children colour their actions with their own particular preferences.

## Time

Movement can be speedy and sudden as well as slow and leisurely, with degrees of progression between the two. Fast and slow are movements which appear early in the understanding of young children who soon become aware that for many of their activities there is an appropriateness of speed. A slow stretching of the leg to find the section of the climbing frame or rung of the ladder which can safely take the weight of the body, a quick dash to get to the ball, and the lively quality of the 'breeze' dance, are all examples of an appropriate use of time in the play of most four- and five-year-olds. In addition to being fast and urgent and slow and leisurely, there are many degrees from one end of the continuum to the other. As children gradually manage to employ more and more of these stages of time, so notions of acceleration and deceleration come into play, featuring prominently in the movement of children around six and seven.

## Flow

Flow refers to movement which ranges from being restricted and bound through to movement which is essentially free and outgoing. Descriptions of young children are often given by adults in terms of flow with phrases such as 'outgoing', 'expansive', 'restrained' or 'withdrawn' giving clues to their behaviour at any given time. As well as being indicative of mood the use of flow also features in the acquisition of skill, for example, in cutting paper, in making models, in learning to write or playing a musical instrument. At first, bound flow, associated with extreme care, reflects tentativeness. But, as skill improves, so does the sense of confidence expressed by the freeing of flow. Activities carried out on agility apparatus involve a range of flow responses, freer flow giving continuity to the activity and restraint, involving the ability to stop and hold back, helping to prevent accidents to the mover and other children in the vicinity.

## Dynamics in context

Dynamic and rhythmic components of movement have no particular value in themselves; what is important is that they are used appropriately. It is 'no better' to be able to colour movement with sudden, quick vitality than with sustainment and leisure. Strong action is 'no better' than a gentle, fine touch. Assessment depends entirely upon the context in which movement occurs although, of course, it is important to have as wide a range as possible in order to make appropriate selections. The purpose of this aspect of movement is extended when children's expressive behaviour is looked at in Chapter 6.

# SPACE: THE MEDIUM IN WHICH MOVEMENT TAKES PLACE

Space is referred to in figure 13 in two ways; first as the personal space surrounding the body, sometimes referred to as the kinesphere (Laban, 1948) and, second, the general space which is beyond personal space and bounded by the particular confines within which any activity takes place. In activities involving agility the general space might be the climbing frame in the garden, swings and roundabouts in the park, the adventure playground, the specially designated section of the nursery school or the gymnasium or movement hall of infant, junior and middle schools. Games-like activities take place in a variety of locations, sometimes with permanent set boundaries but more often with boundaries and obstacles set by children themselves. The needs of dance are for 'uncluttered space' and a 'comfortable floor'.

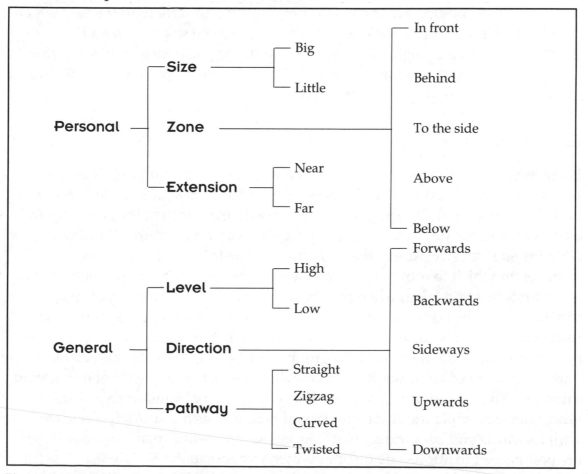

*Figure 13    Space: the medium in which movement takes place*

## Size and extension

In the movement world of young children size is normally associated with extension and so these two elements of personal space are considered here together. In identifying movements which are kept near the body or extend a long way from it, and are large or small, it is easy to conjure up images of children who use such notions frequently. 'Near', 'far', 'big' and 'little' feature prominently in the learning of young children and therefore their experience in this area is vitally important.

## Zone

The structure of the body provides spatial areas of movement with different parts of the body having their 'natural' zones. Young children use their arms a great deal to gesture in the upper areas of space in front of, behind, to the side, and above their bodies. This natural zoning occurs similarly with the legs which step, gesture and jump in the lower regions of personal space. Fun and excitement may be brought about by varying the natural use of zones; moving around with hands grasping ankles and hanging upside down on a ladder are just two such examples of inverted zoning.

## Direction

Direction is a development of zoning. The three bodily dimensions of length, breadth and depth provide the basis of all orientation in space; the length of the body gives rise to the directions of up and down, the width of the body to left and right, and the depth of the body to forwards and backwards. It is obvious from the skeletal structure of the body that forwards is the most natural direction in which to move, and that when babies are able to stand unaided this is the first direction taken when they begin to walk. It is not, however, only the dimensions of the body, but also awareness of different body parts, which help the understanding of direction. Apart from crawling, when the head leads the baby forwards while parallel to the ground, the head is naturally associated with movement of an upward direction while the feet give a sense of downward intention. The sides of the body, together with the arms, familiarise children with sideways while the chest and back of their bodies are strongly associated with forwards and backwards. In encouraging 'dance-like' play young children are best helped to appreciate directions by references to the body with suggestions to 'follow their noses', let their 'elbows lead the way' or their 'heels go first'. Later, when directional awareness is less dependent on reference to their own bodies, children can cope with general suggestions to move in different directions. It is useful to remind ourselves that while in 'dance-like' activity directions can be used freely and creatively, in games-orientated activity direction is employed according to the demands of the particular game being played and, therefore, opportunities for variation are limited. Nevertheless, direction is an important factor in games and games-like activities, first, in action skills such as kicking, hitting and throwing and, later, for the seven- and eight-year-olds, in tactical play.

## Level

Level, or the height at which any action takes place, ranges from low to high with many variations between the two extremes. Levels are personal, in that they are related to the body. Low level is deep and around the floor, medium level is situated approximately at mid-body and the third level is above the head. Young children use these notions often in their play. One well known example is in 'family play' where one child bends the knees and shuffles along at low level, being the baby, while the other walks on toes, or puts on high heeled shoes, in order to 'become' the grown-up and use authority from a higher position. Characteristically, young children enjoy extremes as they move freely or respond to suggestions from adults or friends. They 'know' and delight in the use of high and low as they move while medium level is used less frequently and with less understanding. The 'in between' level is more likely to be passed through *en route* than actively engaged in its own right. Later, in relation to the young child's increasing ability to recognise smaller divisions and to order them sequentially, usually around six years, it assumes greater importance.

## Pathways and patterns

Pathways assume an important role in children's spontaneous play. Three- and four-year-olds mainly travel in straight lines and curves while by about six or seven, children may be expected to respond to challenges to move in all four of the following ways: straight, angular, curved and twisted. Challenging children to move in particular pathways implies considerable knowledge on their part and understanding in this sphere of movement comes about slowly.

The challenge to 'make a straight movement in space' implies:

- no change of direction;
- an uninterrupted pathway;
- a single focus.

The challenge to 'make an angular movement in space' implies:

- movement that changes direction acutely;
- an awareness of sharp angles;
- a zigzag movement.

The challenge to 'make a curved movement in space' implies:

- a directional change which is gradual;
- an awareness of smooth, even, movement and no angularity.

The challenge to 'make a twisted movement in space' implies:

- movement which curves first in one direction and then in another;
- an awareness that movement is going back on itself creating a pattern similar to an 'S' or figure of eight.

Movement patterns such as those seen in track marks left on a treasure hunt, a drawing in a wet sand tray or when dialling a telephone illustrate situations where the movement is two-dimensional in nature. When, however, children move in what might be called 'air space', movement becomes more flexible and three-dimensional. Along with travelling actions across the floor, pathways and patterns in the air, created by gestures of the arms, are an important element of dance. In agility-type activity, floor patterns assume greater significance than air patterns and in some games, but not all, ground pathways are major considerations often coming about by chance according to how the game develops and the kinds of tactics involved.

# RELATIONSHIPS: THE MOVING BODY INTERACTS

## The body relates to itself

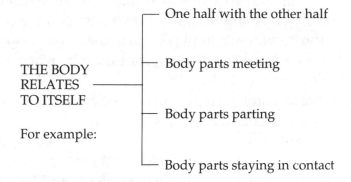

THE BODY
RELATES
TO ITSELF

For example:

— One half with the other half

— Body parts meeting

— Body parts parting

— Body parts staying in contact

*Figure 14　The body relates to itself*

One of the growing excitements for young children comes about through a gradual realisation of the various ways in which different parts of the body relate to one another. Sometimes the relationship occurs between the use of large sections of the body. Figure 15 shows Hannah, aged four, maintaining a strong, wall-like lower half while her top half bends over to look through her legs. Other examples include making a back for someone to jump over, or providing a gap through which to pull a friend. These are relationships between parts of the body which children knowingly create for themselves.

*Figure 15　Looking through legs gives a different perspective*

As a child's awareness of individual body parts increases so too does the sophistication with which these parts relate to each other. In 'dance play', for example, not only may the palms of the hands touch each other as in clapping but sides, backs and fingertips may make contact in a variety of ways. The right hand wrapping round the body to arrive near to, or on, the left shoulder brings about a different expression from the right elbow resting on the right hip. In handling apparatus the body tends to play a participatory and supporting role while specific parts are engaged in action as, for example, when an arm and hand are involved in bouncing a ball.

Relationships between body parts also involve dynamic, rhythmic and spatial nuances. Cartwheels and handstands, for instance, demand refined articulation of the relevant parts of the body and careful spacing between them as the weight is adjusted throughout the activity. Weight adjustment is also important in all sorts of climbing activities where hands and feet work in synchronisation as children travel along, upwards, or downwards. Climbing is an extremely complex business and early attempts are often restrained and slow. It is as though the children are pausing for thought, or collecting themselves, which is, in a sense, what they are doing. As if to help the children on their way adults are sometimes tempted to give physical assistance, even to the extent of lifting the foot of a young child and placing it on the next rung. Helpful as this might seem, the foot is momentarily taken out of the child's control. Consequently, the important changes of body weight, which give significant signals to the child, are temporarily removed. Although the pattern of hand-foot co-ordination is differently sequenced as children become more skilled, the weight adjustment remains central to the activity of climbing itself.

In figure 16, Josh, two-and-a-half years old, shows confidence which can be seen in the lovely, long stretch of his body and the careful placing of hands and feet as he estimates the distance between the rungs. Although, on this occasion, he missed a rung at one point on the way up he resumed climbing almost immediately, his hands and feet easily regaining their former co-ordinated pattern. He also took the opportunity to rest on a conveniently placed flat surface of the climbing frame and to be still after he completed his climb. Action and recovery are natural partners in early childhood activity and children may often be seen in attitudes of repose on agility apparatus. This is absolutely normal, a time to be respected and not to be rushed.

*Figure 16    Hands and feet move simultaneously as distance is estimated*

## The body relates to objects

Activity related to objects which can be moved and manipulated causes the body to behave in different ways from movement related to the stable environment. Children's play with such things as hoops, bats and balls where there is a considerable measure of unpredictability, and where chance happenings frequently dictate the next move, are different in kind. In bouncing a ball against the floor or into the air, for example, effective contact has to be made between the hand and the ball. This is no small feat for very young children and few children under five can manage to keep such an activity going for long. Even greater demands are made when the same activity is carried out with a bat instead of the hand. Now an additional relationship has to be made between the child and the bat in an attempt to make contact with the ball. Contact between objects, in this case a bat and a ball, is brought about by the use of the body in time and space. When the size of the ball is diminished or a narrow stick replaces the bat even greater difficulty is encountered. These areas of progression indicate clearly the complexity of the movement patterns brought into play (see schemas on page 85).

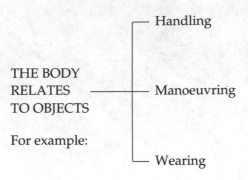

THE BODY
RELATES
TO OBJECTS

For example:

— Handling

— Manoeuvring

— Wearing

*Figure 17   The body relates to objects*

The action of throwing involves not only an appropriate grip but also the ability to 'let go'. A familiar behaviour pattern is that of two-year-olds feeding ducks in the local pond. With careful precision they pull a fairly large piece of bread from the paper bag and with a forward trajectory movement throw it into the pond – rather than to the ducks! They know what they are about, that is, feeding the ducks with bread. But they have some difficulty in releasing the bread at the appropriate moment in space and time to make it happen. After the throw has been achieved fingers often remain taut and extended for several moments before the whole procedure is repeated. Progressively through the next few years children increase their ability to merge the separate stages of the process – preparing to throw, throwing, recovery – into a cohesive and harmonised whole. By the time they reach four or five years of age, children are able to focus clearly and anticipate the end result to the extent of aiming at one duck and throwing the bread to another some way off. At this stage the action has become so well known that an element of play is allowed in. The way in which throwing develops is talked about, and illustrated, in more detail in the following chapter.

In dance, activity related to objects happens less frequently although early experiences will include the handling of balloons, drapes, percussion and other objects and materials. While drapes and dressing-up clothes may assist expressive movement, early childhood workers will recognise how very young children, who usually move with ease and fluency, can suddenly become wooden and stick-like when encouraged to move with a tambourine, hand castanet or set of bells. It is difficult enough to make such instruments extensions of the body but the complexity increases when young children are asked to dance with drum and beater which demands grip from both hands. However, children enjoy moving with percussion instruments, materials, and other objects, and as long as their use is introduced in an informed and sensitive way, and at a time of readiness, they soon become familiar with the extra demands of dancing in this way.

## The body relates to other people

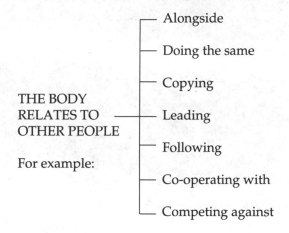

Figure 18    *The body relates to other people*

Associating with others is an integral part of the movement activities of young children. They work alongside others sharing space and equipment, in the sense that they allow it to happen, and, sometimes, when one child initiates an activity two or three others will join in. 'Follow my leader' is a favourite theme and an example of an early, uncomplicated relationship. At its most basic it is a relationship where the followers mainly conform to the track of the leader. This gradually develops so that more and more of the detail of the leader's activity is taken on by the follower and, by the time children reach seven or eight, identical complex sequences are often in evidence.

Children include adults and their peers in negotiating relationships; they climb, pass, travel round, up and over them. Co-operating alongside, and competing against, characterise two more of the social relationships which young children experience. During an activity time together, Callum and his mother have danced, jumped and played football together. In figure 19 on page 24, Callum is seen looking at his mother's feet, 'checking' when she is about to jump so that he can match his jump to hers and take off at the same time.

*Figure 19    Callum watches his mother 'to time' his jump with hers*

## Summary

The main concern of this chapter has been to establish, comment upon, and illustrate the four separate categories of human movement in the ways in which they relate to young children. These categories are closely and intricately related. The following chapters will look in greater detail at integrated patterns of children's activity as they learn to move more effectively and expressively, and move to learn in terms of thinking and socialising.

# 2 LEARNING TO MOVE

From the first moments after birth babies make their needs and feelings known through movement and, through movement, they gather to themselves a whole variety of impressions which help to create an ever-changing picture of their personal world. Right from the start the supporting, sharing, facilitating roles of parents and others are immensely important for the development of the newborn infant.

The main purpose of this chapter is to highlight ways in which movement relates to the physical development of babies and young children as they learn to move in increasingly skilful and versatile ways. It is not always easy to isolate sheer 'physicality' and throughout the chapter the inter-related nature of movement is kept firmly in mind.

The biological processes of growth and maturation become evident soon after birth and their outcomes remain of central interest to parents, family and friends throughout childhood. Early motor responses are common to all babies, (unless damaged) irrespective of gender or culture, and the order in which they appear is equally invariable. For example, co-ordination of large body movements precedes precise and specific movements, and unilateral movement follows the bi-lateral movement which dominates activity in the early months. However, although a set pattern of events is more or less predictable, the rate of development is very much an individual affair and, as we will see later, is to a certain extent associated with appropriate environmental provision.

## 'KNOWLEDGE IN THE MAKING'

Although at first the movement of babies may appear to be relatively gross, and unfocused, almost at once they show clear signs of responding to the peopled world around them. Bower (1977) found, for example, that by two weeks of age a baby can identify both the voice and face of his or her mother. As babies come to recognise the faces of other regularly encountered carers so they enlarge their circle of familiar and friendly contacts. It is usually at about seven months, when faces are appreciated in greater detail, that initial anxiety is expressed when confronted with strange and unfamiliar faces (Roberts, 1981, p. 47). Babies also respond to their own, distinctly felt needs. For example, they make, progressively successful attempts to locate the source of food, to suck, to grasp or to alter the position of the body. Through such body movements as these Gerhardt (1979, p. 1) suggests the young child discovers consistencies which, in turn, create patterns of response. She calls these 'knowledge in the making'.

The ways in which young children manage the length, height, weight and proportions of their bodies as they grow and develop sometimes seem little short of a miracle, particularly as the relationship of the dimensions and proportions of the body changes through the years. As Jackson (1993, p. 28) comments:

> *The vitality and speed of change is astonishing. Growing up is like a complex, fast moving game, where not only the rules and goal posts keep changing but also the players themselves.*

It is vitally important that parents, and those who share in child caring, are aware of the physical changes their children are going through. Only then can they maintain an active part in these games, identifying with, extending and enriching the many experiences which make for flexible and mobile development. Continuing and appropriate involvement of this sort provides important building blocks in the physical, emotional and cognitive make-up of a child. Certainly there is plenty of evidence to connect the early age of so-called criminal activity, which seems to dominate our news, with an early childhood lacking appropriate family interplay.

# EARLY 'HANDLING' EXPERIENCES

The first year of early childhood features a high level of 'handling' on the part of parents and carers, in most cases the highest level throughout childhood. The state of the infant in such handling situations may range from quiet, peaceful sleep to agitated, wakeful activity. Those new to caring for young infants will recognise the varied demands in trying at one time to keep hold of a slippery, wriggling baby and, at another, to handle an intense, non-giving 'ramrod'. The appropriate handling responses are learnt 'on the job' and those involved in constant daily care soon find a familiarity born of practice, knowing 'what' to do and 'how' to do it.

During the early months, parents interact with their babies using a personal range of sophisticated movement 'ingredients' as if to pass on something of their chosen patterns, actions and moods – which, of course, is just what they do. At this stage there is the largest contrast ever to be seen between the variety, skill and refinement of movement with which parents and closely associated carers function and the early, unsophisticated movements of the children they live with and care for.

The period of 'handling play' is an important part of the development of babies and, as such, gives an early start in the appreciation of a rich 'vocabulary of movement'. Being picked up, held upright, put down, turned over, made comfortable, are just a few of the many handling activities which take place daily and which babies come to recognise and contribute to themselves. At times specific parts of the handler's body may take on importance and come to have special meaning; the hands that stretch out, the arms that hold and the lips that kiss. Here again babies contribute, activating their bodies as arms come towards them and pursing their lips to share a kiss. On other occasions it is the expressive quality colouring a given action which makes an impression, rather than the parts of the handler's body being brought into play or the action itself. Young infants can feel and respond to the difference between, for example, the strength and firmness of a lift, the gentleness of a caress and the vitality of a succession of lively, facial gestures especially designed to make them laugh.

Not only can young infants respond knowingly to an increasing number of people they see around them and to whom they relate, but they can also begin to recognise individuals by hearing them rather than by seeing them move. The light, crisp steps of one, the heavy, regular tread of another and the rapid patter of a third, for example, come across as distinct dynamic patterns associated with particular individuals who currently inhabit their world.

## Expressive interaction

As suggested earlier, adults have developed, to a greater or lesser degree, a vast range of movement 'ingredients' which they can mix and match to suit particular occasions. It is from this extensive movement repertoire that appropriate expression of voice and bodily gesture can be selected when interacting with young children. For example, in responding to a young infant who is fractious and ill at ease, a quiet, soothing tone, accompanied by a rocking or stroking action (involving the movement elements of sustainment and gentleness) may often have a positive effect. The success of this expressive exercise on the part of the handler is seen first in the sharing, by the infant, in the newly created mood of calm and, second, in the retention of that mood. In a similar way, a short, brisk and lively movement and tone of voice used in a time of shared playfulness produces a different mood in the young infant and is invigorating rather than soothing in effect. The 'impressive' nature of movement as identified in these situations is an important concept within the work of Laban and is one which will be elaborated later.

## To move appropriately is a sign of development

It is interesting to note that an appropriate selection of movement ingredients is not always readily available to young brothers and sisters for they will still be developing their own personal framework of movement and can only approximate to what is needed. The well-intentioned kiss of a young brother or sister can be rough, the cuddle too tight and the rocking of the push-chair too vigorous. Encouragement is needed for them to acquire the appropriate 'movement mix', an encouragement which has to extend beyond immediate directions of 'not too rough' or 'not too tight' or 'steadily'. Acting appropriately means being able to respond to perceived needs. This is particularly relevant in the case of using movement, whether in terms of functional activity or as a means of expression. To move appropriately is a sign of increasing development, and young siblings and friends, anxious to be involved in a caring role, need help not only in recognising what is needed but also in selecting from their own movement repertoire in relation to that need. Like all areas of learning, consolidation is an important factor in development, and thus the use of a range of gentle dynamics in stroking a rabbit, treading heavily in order to leave footprints in the sand, and squeezing paint from a resistant tube, all have relevance here. Domestic play – wheeling trolleys, building towers, setting out cups and saucers, dressing, undressing and rocking dolls and 'being the baby' – all play an important role in understanding what is needed in the 'real life' situation.

# Early rhythmic play

## Accents and emphasis

It is interesting to watch how adults playing with their babies use varying emphasis, or accent in their games. As well as individual favourites, a common example is where someone makes a movement starting some way away from the baby which, as it gets nearer and nearer, gathers speed and force and culminates in a moment of impact and excitement as the baby is picked up. Often some sound or nonsense 'word play' accompanies this game and is an integral part of it. Starting from nothing and gradually gathering force and

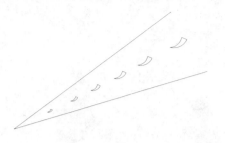

*Figure 20    Impactive movement with stress at the end of the phrase (Davies, 1994)*

energy in this way is an example of impactive movement and sound. When thisrhythmic play becomes well established the baby begins to anticipate and to share its distinctive patterning.

Conversely, another well-known rhythmical game starts as the baby is lifted into the air with a strong, emphatic flourish which gradually fades away to nothing when he or she is lowered with decreasing speed and force. This movement pattern which explodes and then diminishes, again often accompanied by sound, is an example of impulsive movement.

*Figure 21    Impulsive movement with stress at the start of the phrase (Davies, 1994)*

## Developing shared play

A variety of movement play along these lines, with accents placed at different instances along the stream of activity, gives the young infant an early experience of 'shared' rhythmical phrasing. Figure 22, on page 30, shows Sanna and her baby of three months enjoying a period of rhythmic play together. Sanna employs a rich range of bodily and qualitative movement when she plays with Aarne. Until now she has been mainly lifting and lowering him on her lower leg, an activity he has come to know and to enjoy. This is the first time their

Figure 22    *Early rhythmic play*

Figure 23    *'Going between': parental rhythms are shared*

rhythmic play has taken on this particular pattern and in contrast to his previous, familiar activity he is clearly not yet at ease.

Rhythmic play of this kind continues to be important for some time. Charlotte, aged eighteen months, is seen in figure 23 (on page 30) enjoying being passed between her parents. Her own contribution is considerable as she anticipates and shares in the sensation of being passed, or gently thrown, by one and received by the other. Charlotte has learnt to recognise the different movement messages given to her by each of her parents. She participates in their individual and joint rhythms and expresses her own.

*Figure 24    Learning to launch*

Alexandra, who is three, also enjoys periods of rhythmic play. Her anticipation and contribution to these take on a more complex form than Charlotte's. In order to jump into her father's arms in figure 24 (page 31) she makes a circuit of climbing and travelling on the agility frame to arrive at the steps from which she takes off each time. (This familiar 'route-taking' is referred to again on page 59.) First steadying herself on the steps, and as if to jump, she puts out her arms and leans forward towards her father who puts his arms round her waist and lifts her high into the air. She does not quite have either the understanding or the physical power of propulsion necessary to jump from the steps, although all the signs show that this will soon follow. With lots of jumping experience to come, by watching her six-year-old brother jump from the top step, high into the air before being caught, and with the continuing support of her father, she will soon be able to launch herself into his arms.

It is useful for parents and 'handlers' to check occasionally that the movement phrases they use when interacting with their young children are sufficiently varied. Most adults have preferred movement patterns which they use to communicate and by which they become well known. In terms of speaking too, parents may recognise themselves as either those who prefer sentence construction which is impulsively structured (with the momentum at the start of the sentence), or who are impactive in their articulation (making the end of the sentence a punch-line). Such individually pronounced, and often repeated, associated movement and speech patterns are the stuff of impersonations both for professional entertainment and at the more amateur level of family 'take-offs'. Such occasions alert us, sometimes for the first time, to just how pronounced and habitual our movement and speech make-up really is. They also show how our movement and speech patterns are picked up by our children. As North (1972, p. 6) writes:

> *Young children respond spontaneously to the movement of another person – 'see' or 'feel' or 'experience' the person as a whole, through their whole being with a kinaesthetic sense, without analysing or verbalising...*

# On-going movement development

From the basic, reflex actions of sucking, swallowing and grasping, which characterise both pre-natal and post-birth activity, come a whole range of sensory-motor actions. These follow each other in rapid succession during the first two years and are mainly concerned with postural control, manipulation, balance and locomotion. All the time, as babies grow and develop, they delight those around by adding new actions which they constantly repeat, varying them and combining them in different ways. These 'schemas of action' are described by Athey (1990, p. 36) as 'patterns of repeatable actions that lead to early categories and then to logical classifications'. Two further definitions of schemas, which are particularly helpful in this context, are given by Neisser (1976, p. 111) who describes them as 'dynamic, active, information-seeking structures', and by Piaget and Inhelder (1973, p. 382) who suggest that the function of a schema is to enable generalisations to be made about objects and events in the environment to which a schema is applied.

The actions carried out by babies and young children are many and varied, curtailed only by the relatively confined areas in which they take place such as the cot, the carry cot, the highchair, on the rug or in the bath. It is at this active, but zone-restricted stage that family and friends can be heard to advise first-time parents with such words as 'wait until he is moving around' or 'you soon won't be able to leave her alone for a minute'. What such well meaning friends are predicting, of course, is the number of new and more complex actions young children add to their collections as soon as they can reach many more things in an increasingly accessible environment. It is at this stage that the needs for safety and opportunity coincide. While ensuring a stimulating and opportunity-filled environment we need to be careful not to leave potentially harmful materials and obstacles in the way of young children.

In terms of development young children not only increase the number of actions they can do but also develop and refine the skill with which those actions are carried out. Improved skill acquisition comes about partly through repetition in a familiar situation, for example climbing stairs or steps over and over again, and partly through adapting a particular action by trying it out in a variety of different situations as when climbing takes place in relation to garden walls, trees and ropes.

Although movement development is still generally linear and predictable, as is shown in the way children acquire motor skills, it would be a mistake to envisage that maturation alone is totally responsible for such development. Exposure to a wide selection of environmental opportunities plays an important part in the developmental process and as Brierley (1987, p. 3) advises, a good environment is not a luxury but a necessity during the early years of life. It may be helpful at this stage to be more specific and to look in some detail at the development of two quite different actions. There are many interesting and important actions which could be used as illustrations here and it is difficult to make a choice. Balancing is an early activity and, as one which is kept in active use throughout life, is perhaps a particularly good one to consider. Throwing, although different in kind, is also a life-long activity and, therefore, also appropriate to include.

## Balance

Balance involves activity where the centre of gravity is in a constant state of change. It is therefore an essential constituent of locomotive and manipulative skills. As children travel through the various stages of balance control, the provision of stimulating environmental challenges, as well as interaction with parents, teachers and friends, is all important. It is through such provision and accompanying conversation that a well educated and finely tuned body emerges. On the other hand, lack of appropriate provision can result at best in less than articulate movers and, at worst, in children who are physically inept, lack bodily confidence and who, sadly, are in danger of being overlooked or even bullied.

### Standing

Although the many and varied ways in which babies gradually achieve balance, and engage in early forms of movement across the floor, are of great interest, the attention and degree of delight given to the first attempts of a young child to stand unaided are perhaps without match. At first the arms and hands are held away from the body and used in a mobile way, almost as regulatory wings. And, initially, for a short period, eyes are often cast down as if to make sure the ground stays where it is. But once their balance is mastered young children are able to view the world from a more or less vertical stance. This means getting used to things and people being differently positioned. Objects, family and friends originally looked at from below change to being seen mainly to the front or to the side. It undoubtedly feels quite different for young children to be this way up for long periods of time as, in the words of Gerhardt (1973, p. 21), they 'align the world in relation to this new verticality'.

### The furniture walkabout

As proficiency in standing develops, the well known 'furniture walkabout' becomes a much practised and familiar activity. It is important that when familiarity is established to such a degree that mis-judgements rarely or never occur, and the walkabout is an assured activity, significant changes in the position and relationship of furniture can be made. These changes, calling for a different perception and movement response, will at first be fairly large and obvious, perhaps 'swopping' the positions of a stool and highchair. Dynamic equilibrium is dependent upon a sensing of body awareness which becomes increasingly detailed as finer adjustments of balance are called for. Later on, smaller and less obvious furniture moves can be included until young children can cope with all the challenges presented and are able, quite literally, to 'take everything in their stride'. The day in which young children make the transition, albeit only momentarily, from dependence on people or furniture to taking first steps without support is hailed as a red letter day in the family circle (Roberts, 1981, p. 78). But she suggests a great deal of practice is needed, in terms of balancing, co-ordinating and control of speed and direction, for the further development of this newly emerging skill. To manage to do something once or twice is no guarantee of permanent skill acquisition but, as Bruce (1987, p. 49) writing with reference to Bruner's notion of 'scaffolding', suggests, 'because a child cannot "perform", or can only perform falteringly, does not mean that he/she is not ready for the task'.

## Walking

Gradually, as progress in early locomotion is made, the balancing role of the arms is reduced and eventually disappears. Meanwhile tottering and walking, involving feedback from skeletal, muscular and neurological systems, are added to the child's repertoire. Once children begin to walk there are tremendous changes in the quality of the walking movement. At first, walking is a stagger from place to place (Thomas, J., Lee, A., Thomas, K., 1988, p. 39). Eventually, those children who are secure and 'at home' in their newly acquired locomotive skills show a high degree of confidence, and associated emotional stability, which can be detected in the easy and unrestricted way (free flow and bodily fluency) with which they move. There will be other children who may also have added the action of walking to their movement repertoire but who move in a disjointed and less fluid way. Usually all that is needed at this early stage is help to achieve greater fluency and 'togetherness'. Additional time and commitment spent on this phase now is a good investment for the future, as the ability to move around freely, and at will, provides fresh opportunities to explore the environment. This, in turn, brings about a vast extension of learning experiences. A consideration of these and other environmental experiences will be provided in Chapter 4.

## Running

In terms of progression it is not such a far cry from walking to running, an activity which often emerges within the domain of a playful game. Excitement and eagerness to get to an enticing object or situation such as a hand proffering a toy, or to get away from a father in 'friendly pursuit', may well provide the necessary stimulus to 'run' (in which instance a free flow forward propulsion may best describe the form of locomotion which comes about). Zaichkowsky, Zaichkowsky and Martinek, (1980, p. 39) describe it in the following way:

> *The initial pattern resembles a hurried walk and is readily seen when a child of about eighteen months attempts to 'run' when playfully pursued. This is not a genuine run, since the child does not have sufficient balance or leg strength to allow both feet to leave the ground momentarily.*

Eventually, locomotion develops into the 'genuine run' referred to here during which children incorporate a brief moment of flight into their action. This is a significant development which, because of the initial brevity of being airborne, is sometimes overlooked. As legs become stronger so the length of the stride increases, replacing the rise and fall features of the previous stage. The use of the arms changes character too. Unfocused, roundabout pathways become straight backwards-forwards ones which now occur in opposition to the movement of the legs.

At around five or six years, with an easy and smooth action in place, children are into real running. At this stage the action schema of running is extended through notions of speed, distance and endurance – how fast, how far and for how long.

Just as early stages of walking involve instances of tottering and falling, early stages of running often result in grazed knees and bloody noses! The establishment of walking and running behaviour is welcomed by parents and educators of all kinds as a significant stage of development and associated maturity. As Gallahue (1983) comments:

> *The movement patterns of walking and running are basic to our everyday activities. It is essential that they be developed to the mature level . . .*

### Development at different rates

It is important to remind ourselves that at this stage a minority of children may show signs of some degree of impairment or delay in their motor development, sometimes referred to as clumsiness. Should such diagnosis be made, specialist help should be sought early on. In January 1994, Action Research, a medical research charity, published a leaflet of advice to parents with children suffering from dyspraxia, the name given to this co-ordination disorder. Attention is drawn, among other symptoms, to problems of balance and movement co-ordination which, they point out, diminish ability to cope with everyday life. Referring to the 'hidden' disorder of a clumsy child, the report suggests that as many as five to ten per cent of children fall into this category. This supports the earlier findings of Groves (1979) who indicated that five per cent of children at school experience motor problems and that there is likely to be at least one 'physically awkward' child in every primary school class. In quite a different context, and with reference to another minority group, Nielsen (1992, p. 43) draws attention to the ways in which gross motor activity such as that seen in running is replaced. She writes:

> *Instead of experimenting with how far and how fast it is possible to run and instead of preferring running to walking, many blind children fulfil their need for gross motor activity by jumping on the same spot or by experimenting with tiptoeing . . .*

## Balance adjustment

Returning once again to ways in which most children continue to explore their environment we see that balancing adjustments are called for time and time again as, for example, when carrying an ice cream, turning a corner, balancing along a wall, or when walking on icy roads. This is illustrated by the way in which Hannah, aged four, 're-adopts' the use of her arms as she manoeuvres the ball with her feet in figure 25 (page 38). Notice too, the direct focus on her activity and the signs of bound flow quality which is frequently seen when children try out new activities.

While encouragement of a comfortable and effective level of dynamic balance is essential for the movement development of all children, there is no doubt that some are better at balancing feats than others and display a particular and ongoing interest in this aspect of movement expertise. Sometimes, these children go on to exploit their particular interest or skill in terms of amateur or professional activities such as skateboarding, ice skating, skiing, rock climbing, and other kinds of physical challenges, where a reduced base for balance and the need to adapt to a changing environment are constant demands. Such interests, either in terms of active participation or as a spectator sport, often become life-long pursuits and in these, as in earlier stages of balance, the kinaesthetic sense, 'knowing by a bodily feel', is constantly in evidence.

*Figure 25    Arms come into play when new balancing skills are needed*

# Throwing

Throwing is a complex activity in which several parts of the body move simultaneously as they cope with the release and propulsion of an object of some kind. Like balancing, throwing is an early activity in the behaviour of babies and, similarly, as a developed skill, is used in a variety of life-long situations. The order of skill acquisition in this action is progressive but the amount of time it takes to achieve a fluent and effective action varies with individual children. Only the major ingredients of throwing are discussed here but many more detailed analyses exist and the attention to detail given by Robertson and Halverson (1984, pp. 102–115) and Thomas, Lee and Thomas (1988, pp. 42–45) will be particularly useful for readers wishing to know more about this important activity.

### Eighteen months to three years

Between approximately eighteen months and three years, the throwing action starts mainly at the elbow with the body facing the direction in which the throw is to take place. The weight of the child's body at the point of release is either forward or backward (usually forward) with rarely any body adjustment happening during the action. The widely extended fingers which accompany the release of the object is a well-known phenomenon at this phase and best observed when children feed ducks at the pond or throw pebbles into the sea.

It is well illustrated in figure 26 (page 40) by Laura, aged two-and-a-half, who has just thrown some gravel from one part of the path to another.

## Three to six years

In the next phase, usually between three and six years of age, the major difference in throwing is indicated by the way the whole body shows gradual signs of co-ordinated action. As the arm is swung diagonally backward and the elbow is flexed, so the trunk turns in preparation for the throw. Although the body weight is often brought forward as the throwing action takes place, in many cases the forward step is taken on the same side as the throwing arm and although the fingers are not necessarily extended at the moment of release the throwing arm simply continues its arc downward and forward. Underarm throwing also features prominently as shown in figure 27 (page 40) by William. He is well co-ordinated and his 'same arm, same leg' stance is typical of three-year-olds.

## The older child

When the technique of throwing matures, fluent and effective co-ordination of the body is marked. For example, as the throwing arm is swung backward in preparation so the body rotates and the other arm is raised in complementary balance. With the weight of the body on the back foot the whole body is in a state of articulate preparation. From here the throw is achieved with a strong, spatially directed movement accompanied by a forward step on the opposite foot. Benjamin, aged seven, shown in figure 28 (page 40), is well on the way to achieving skilled action.

## The importance of throwing and catching

Throwing and catching are essential ingredients of children's play. Not to master these twin activities is to deny access to endless hours of solitary and group play of both a co-operative and competitive nature. It is worthwhile, therefore, to spend time and imagination in providing the right sorts of experiences at appropriate stages in order for children to have a good initiation in this area of movement. Some children will excel in this type of activity and proceed to make games a major interest in their lives needing, at first, little more than the apparatus and friends in the way of external motivation. However, a basic proficiency in these activities is the right of all children if they are to take part alongside their peers without the fear of being singled out as someone who cannot throw or catch – and consequently left out of the game and the camaraderie which accompanies it. There will be a comfortable time later on when children can rationalise their own wishes to opt out of games for good

*Figure 26    Early throwing pattern ending in outstretched hand*

*Figure 27    Same arm, same leg – a typical throwing action*

*Figure 28    The whole body prepares to throw*

reasons of their own. To be able to do this from the level of a basic competence is far better than for reasons of inadequacy.

Throwing, catching and balancing are just three examples of what are referred to by Arnold (1988, p. 128) as 'pre-requisite skills'. He describes a person unable to kick, trap, dribble and pass as someone unable to participate successfully in soccer, a game where such skills are fundamental ingredients. There is no doubt about the authenticity of this claim and many instances of reluctance on the part of the children to join in can be traced to non-existent or low level skills. Seen from the child's point of view, feelings of ineptitude are made worse by the knowledge that his or her presence in a team bent on a lively and effective game, and a victory, is unwelcome. In identifying distance and deviance in the context of play and the culture of childhood, Brown (in Moyles, ed. 1994, p. 61) comments that:

> the ability to operate successfully within the society of children can be seen to depend upon performance in play and its associated activities.

He goes on to refer to the sense of rejection felt by children who are isolated when their performance of a chosen activity is judged unsatisfactory by a group.

In the first instance, however, pre-requisite skills exist in the form of singular, or co-ordinated, skills in their own right. At this early stage they are not pre-requisites for anything more than responding to immediate challenges posed by the environment or self. The emergence and development of basic skills are evident in the variety of activities in which young children engage in the first eight years of life and for which they show a considerable appetite.

## A young appetite for movement

Children have a natural appetite for movement, an appetite which requires as much consideration and attention as their appetites for food, drink, rest and sleep. We have only to walk onto a beach, go into a park, wait at a bus stop, or be anywhere in the company of young children, to sense what is meant by movement being a common denominator of all activity and a 'must' in their lives. Wherever our gaze rests, young children can be observed demonstrating their natural interest in moving, their physical need and motivation to move. The frequency and intensity may vary, but the nature and purpose of the activity remain constant factors. To deny, or seriously restrict, opportunities for children to move is now a relatively rare occurrence but where it happens the results are predictable and sad. However, it may be because the ill effects of poor or inappropriate movement provision are less obvious than in other more immediately life-sustaining areas, that it receives insufficient attention from some providers in home, care or school settings.

The interest that children display in moving falls into four distinct but inter-related categories.

- Relating their bodies to the stable environment through such actions as clambering, climbing, swinging, and balancing.

- Testing themselves in terms of strength and acrobatic and athletic mobility as they roll, tumble, leap and land.

- Testing themselves in terms of dexterity through handling and playing with objects such as rattles, balls, hoops, ropes, sticks and stones.

- Enjoying movement for its own sake in the turning, spinning, twirling, swooping activities which appear spontaneously from time to time.

## 1  Movement activity related to the stable environment

Movement in this category is related to the relatively permanent features of the physical environment through which young children gain experience, knowledge, and understanding of their immediate surroundings and of themselves. To start with they climb people, furniture and household features such as stairs and steps, graduating to railings, fences and trees. They balance along the edges of carpet, kerbstones and walls, swing round bannisters, lamp-posts and overhanging branches of trees, somersault over traffic barriers and jump on, off, over and round anything and everything in sight. It is interesting to observe that even situations which might appear to adults to be inappropriate, uninspiring or even barren for the pursuit of movement are perceived quite differently by children – by Jane for example.

Jane, aged two, was the only child at a small family picnic in Richmond Park. The picnic spot was away from trees and water and, being flat, offered no opportunities for tumbling and rolling. As her mother and her friend talked, the only challenge for Jane was in the form of her own push-chair and for half an hour Jane used this as her climbing frame to step on, climb, balance, twist, turn and jump from. The push-chair, until now her form of transport which by its very nature restricted activity, had become a stimulus for movement. Jane's prolonged spate of activity showed a wide variety of action schemas being performed on one object (Foss, 1974, pp. 208–209).

This use of a variety of schemas was also typical of Amandip's situation although the level of his performance was at a more advanced level. Amandip, aged seven, visiting his grandmother, found the four steps with a hand rail at one side, which led to the front of the house, a haven of experimentation. The structure of the 'domestic playground' presented endless possibilities for running, jumping, hanging, swivelling and swinging. He set himself increasingly difficult challenges which, when mastered, were shown and explained with pride to the family gathering before he set off again on the next round of self-challenging feats.

## 2   The mobile and acrobatic use of the body

From early on young infants spend time using their bodies to bend, stretch, twist, turn and roll in a seemingly endless variety of ways. Sometimes this is for a specific purpose, such as reaching for an object. At other times it is for no apparent reason at all other than the bodily satisfaction experienced. By the time children are secure in standing upright, a much wider canvas for experimentation presents itself and now they try out their bodies in self-chosen, inventive feats of strength, mobility, dexterity and speed.

*Figure 29   Ryan's hands are well-positioned to take his body weight*

At this stage children can be seen rolling down grassy slopes, attempting to take weight on their hands, walking upside-down on all fours, and jumping high and far across real or imagined obstacles. For hours on end such play takes place, sometimes satisfying personal goals but often caught up in group activity where every one is pursuing the same or similar ends. In Figure 29 on page 43 the action of Ryan, aged six, presupposes many, many hours spent putting his hands on the floor and kicking up his feet, before achieving that much longed for, single moment of inverted balance. Consider how much his balance has developed from the time, four or so years ago, when he first conquered being the right way up!

## 3    Handling objects and making them move

This area of movement activity, perhaps more than any other, represents the largest proportion of a young child's movement play. The gripping, shaking, releasing, dropping and throwing of toys, and other assorted objects, are well-known phenomena of young behaviour. Even early signs of 'team play' may be detected in the way in which an adult is actively involved in picking up the toy from the floor so that the game of dropping or throwing may take place again – and again! Setting things in motion, keeping things in motion and stopping things in motion are dominant movement schemas of early childhood and provide delight for most children involved in such activity. The quantity of handling experience which children seek for themselves is a reflection of their seemingly insatiable appetite for movement of this type: wherever they happen to be they always appear to find something 'at hand' or 'at foot' to activate. Such appetites linger on, for the empty drink can on the path and the pebble on the shore lure the hands and feet not only of children but also of accompanying adults.

Handling activities such as these take longer to develop than the first two groups of movement activity. This is due, at least in part, to dependence upon the development of motor skills and eye-hand/eye-foot co-ordination as well as immature concepts of space and time. However, far from putting this type of activity to one side, it is all the more important to provide a wide range of appropriate experiences as early as possible. If children have handled objects of different weights, lengths and sizes – pebbles, balls, sticks, bats and ropes – they are more likely to cope with the activities and games lessons which provide the follow-up work in infant and junior schools. Although a three-year-old may not be able to receive and hit a ball thrown by an adult, a game where a ball is 'directed', almost 'placed', on to the bat is meaningful not just as a preparation for 'real games' to be experienced in the junior school but as a spontaneous game of fun and for getting into the swing of things.

John, aged six, provides us with an interesting example in figure 30. While on holiday he was trying his hand at shooting into a net attached to a pole. It was one of two nets placed at different heights to allow for varying ages and stages of skill. As he walked across to the play area with his father and friends John commented that he had managed to get the ball into the lower net seven times the day before and into the higher net once. He then proceeded to practise shooting at the lower net again while his father used the higher one. John watched his father bending his knees and 'lining up' his body as he prepared to 'shoot' and this was something which John then incorporated into his own shots. This was a productive situation where John practised his own game

*Figure 30    The release of functional action into expressive behaviour*

alongside his father while exchanging 'in context' talk as they went along. Having scored a goal, John was delighted with his success and, as we can see from the photograph, released the narrow alignment of his body taken up while shooting, into a wide expressive gesture.

## 4   The expressive use of the body

Sometimes, young children do not seek the challenge of the stable environment, of performing acrobatic tricks, or of making things move, but instead choose to engage in movement for its own sake and to use it expressively. In the very young it may be seen in the waving, beating and shaking of arms; in slightly older children the equally spontaneous activities of gliding, leaping, whirling, swirling and fluttering. Children may show anger when misunderstood, gentleness when looking after 'the patient' while excitement of any kind can make them shiver, shake or gesticulate excitedly. Children spinning together for the sheer enjoyment of the sensation it gives, moving to music being played, or donning a crown and 'becoming' a king are all examples of childrens' expressive movement. Sometimes they join in with the rhythmic breaking of the waves on the shore or the sound of a car as it takes a bend at speed. Such activities are the stuff of dance and, as such, form the basis of dance experiences given at home, in nursery, infant and junior schools, or during classes in the local dancing school.

*Figure 31    Sisters dancing together*

## The movement curriculum in early childhood education

This four-fold classification of activities, in which young children frequently engage of their own free will, represents the informal and formal movement curriculum associated with early childhood and school settings, and which ideally extends and structures learning of this kind. The children's climbing, swinging and balancing activities find their place, along with their acrobatic skills, within gymnastics. Early experiences in making objects move are developed further in games and athletics while the children's expressive movement is catered for in dance. The differentiated provision schools make for movement education of all kinds is of the utmost importance for it is only when early learning experiences are matched and extended with appropriately challenging provision that we can hope to achieve the best possible movement heritage for our children.

## The responses of very young children

Before we get to that stage, and for very young children, however, the lines between the separate types of activities are blurred and the responses they make to external structures and the structure of their own bodies are complex. Whitehead (1990, p. 115) gives a movement-stressed example of a small child dragging chairs into a line and calling them a train while simultaneously enjoying the physical pleasure of climbing on and off them. A similar example, but one which this time starts with the movement itself, is of a four-year-old girl who, wearing a 'yachting' cap climbs to the top of the frame, where she operates as the captain looking out to sea, while organising her crew below. She enjoys the activity of climbing which enables her to reach the 'look out' as well as the dramatic play which follows. This experience straddles the functional activity of climbing and the expressive play associated with being captain and it is difficult to know which of these concerns prompted the other. In essence, they belong totally together as a unique experience, which Whitehead (1990, p. 173) describes in this way:

> *Symbolic activities are particularly interesting for the early-years educator because they are the fusion of the unique personal experiences and concepts of the individual with the shared systems of shared meanings specific to the culture.*

## SUMMARY

Attention has focused on ways in which children physically manage their bodies in tandem with their development. A range of activities characterising their natural appetite for movement has been identified, through which their evolving movement vocabulary is extended. Following the argument being made throughout this book that the development of movement requires as much consideration and knowledge as other more obvious aspects of early learning, subsequent chapters will look at appropriate provision and enablement.

# 3 MOVING TO LEARN

As suggested in Chapter 2, nowhere is movement, as a common denominator of human functioning, more apparent than in the lives of young children. To undervalue movement when observing children in any context is to miss a central aspect of functioning. It is difficult to describe even the least physical activities of babies and young children without mentioning action, rhythm, or spatial orientation. Similarly, in order to understand the accounts children give of their activities it is important to note such things as what took place in terms of action, how they related to others, what pathway they took and at what level they moved.

Although clearly able to appreciate ways in which movement and physical development are linked with regard to for example, balancing and throwing, many people find 'moving and thinking' and 'moving and feeling' less familiar and accessible notions. At best, these ideas are intuitively sensed while, as implied earlier, they mainly remain unexplored and untested. However, once it is accepted that movement is inextricably linked with *cognitive* (intellectual) functioning and *affective* (emotional) functioning, and that these evolve along similar lines as movement and physical development, then opportunities for providing, supporting and analysing children's activities within an integrated framework become much more feasible.

Movement permeates the complex process of early growth and development unifying the physical, cognitive, emotional and social aspects of life. Movement belongs to them all and they belong to each other. The way in which they are viewed or presented at any given time is simply a matter of emphasis.

## MOVEMENT AND THINKING

Attention was drawn earlier to a lack of available resources and guidelines for the recognition and nurture of early movement development in comparison with those, for instance, related to literacy and numeracy. As we turn now to look at ways in which movement is linked with cognitive, emotional and social functioning there is a similar lack of support. This is not so apparent in some subject-based literature where well-known and prestigious writing has guided curriculum content through a series of changing scenes. There are numerous cases made for the recognition of the important part movement plays in cognitive development and these should not be underestimated. The lack is rather in terms of hard evidence underlying the variety of beliefs and claims made, as well as substantial links with current educational and psychological theory.

The National Association for the Education of Young Children (NAEYC), in their suggestions for developmentally appropriate practice for children aged between five and eight years, claim that physical activity is vital for children's cognitive growth. They stress the need for physical actions to help them grasp abstract concepts, (1987, p. 63). Engagement in active rather than passive activities is emphasised by Katz and Chard (1989) as an important underlying principle of primary education. Both the NAEYC and Katz and Chard imply a concern for what is considered valuable in terms of education. They make judgements about how they think things should be. In each case what they write is evaluative accounting rather than descriptive of what takes place (Arnold, 1988, p. 7).

In much of the literature, however, references to 'associated cognitive and movement development' are relatively general compared with other areas of learning and little has been written in respect of specific concepts. Movement, which is so minutely documented in the area of motor development and skill acquisition, appears as the poor relation here. Considering that general characteristics, or common threads, of cognitive development can be identified in a wide variety of subjects it is difficult to understand why movement features so little in educational texts. Although some educationalists include movement within their brief it is interesting, nevertheless, to note the tendency for that particular chapter to appear at, or near, the end of books dealing with the curriculum whether this refers to nursery, infant, junior or secondary education.

Zaichkowsky, Zaichkowsky and Martinek (1980, p. 11) make a case that through movement and play children learn more than motor skills. They suggest that children:

- learn to employ cognitive strategies;

- understand themselves in psychological terms;

- learn how to interact with other children.

The role of 'action' in relation to 'thought' has been central in most literature since Piaget defined thought as internalised action (Piaget, 1971, pp. 139–46). He wrote:

*The life of the mind is a dynamic reality and intelligence a real and constructive activity.*

In attempting to establish cognitive development within the sphere of movement, examples will be related, where possible to a Piagetian framework. In spite of recent reservations about Piaget's work, modified adherence to his theories is expressed by many educationalists such as Athey (1990), Bruce (1987, 1991), Matthews (1994) and Nutbrown (1994). However, in relating movement to stages of cognitive development, and in referring to specific concepts, there is no intention to 'force a fit' with Piaget's work. Willig (1990, p. 184) suggests that it is often a matter of chance which concepts attract attention and which do not but, arguably, it may be that subjects with tangible outcomes, such as a piece of writing, a model or a painting, have significant advantages over movement where both the process and the end product lack permanence. Perhaps a review of pertinent literature would identify the different key attractions in various areas of learning, a subject worth considering in itself and perhaps particularly so in relation to movement.

# A RESEARCH PROJECT

Before considering specific concepts within children's movement activities it may be helpful to look at a piece of research which I carried out to investigate whether stages of cognitive development could be identified through movement. I found that children between the ages of five and eleven years were able to see similarities (classify), order differences (seriate) and compose in movement reflecting the stages put forward by Piaget (1953), Piaget and Inhelder (1956, 1958), Inhelder (1962) and Inhelder and Piaget (1964). The findings also suggested that not only did the children reach these stages but that, using movement based on their own experiences, they did so earlier than with the traditional test material featuring shape, size and colour.

As part of the research programme, and of particular relevance here, was a movement test which was designed to investigate children's ability, at the ages of five, seven and eleven years, to carry out the following:

- to invent an activity based on given activities;

- to repeat it;

- to hold it in mind while describing it;

- to dissect it;

- to reverse it.

## Setting up the programme

Climbing, balancing and jumping were chosen as the movement ingredients for the test. These were known to be within the capabilities of all the subjects and recognised as the three most commonly used actions by children between five and eleven years old. Further safeguards included a visit by all the children to a common venue where they both experienced all three actions themselves and observed them being carried out by a student. The children were then asked to make up an activity where there was some balancing, some jumping and some climbing and to make it something they could do over and over again. While this test was formally conducted for research purposes, it was based on, and carried out through, 'child-familiar' activities – activities defined by Bruce (1987, p. 135) as embedded in meaning.

## The programme in action

After they had time to become acclimatised to the situation in which they were working, and to make up their activities, the children were individually asked to talk about them in the following ways:

- to describe them without looking at the apparatus;

- to comment on isolated parts of their activity and to select parts from the whole;

- to reverse the order of their actions.

General findings showed that there were significant differences between the three age groups and no difference between the achievements of boys and girls. First, the children were asked in the absence of the apparatus to describe their activity and this presented some problems for nearly all the five-year-olds. Seated at a table facing the tester and with their backs to the apparatus, nearly all the younger subjects turned round to look at the specific place where their activity had taken place in order to give an answer. Even when at a later stage, and with the apparatus in full view this time, they were asked for a description several of them got up from their chair, approached the apparatus and, in some cases, touched it illustrating a need to identify the movement context visually in order to recall with accuracy. In turning to look at the specific place where they had been working, or making physical contact through touch, the younger children seemed to be 're-visiting' the familiarised context which made 'human sense to them' (Donaldson, 1979, p. 25).

The next questions the children were asked referred to their ability to:

- look at parts of their activity in relation to other parts;

- describe what came before or after something else;

- describe how it all began;

- describe how it came to an end.

Carrying their actions in their heads and selecting passages at will, as well as illustrating thought after internalised action appeared within the grasp of the majority of seven- and eleven-year-olds, while only a few of the five-year-olds came near to this level of functioning.

The final test of mentally reversing their actions, that is, to start with their last action and trace their actions backwards to the beginning, found a drop of a third in the seven-year-old range. This is difficult to equate with their earlier success. However, on reflection, it might be argued that the movements and their transitions which made up their various activities had a natural flow from one to the next which lost their inherent logic in reverse order. The movement feeling and, in Donaldson's terms, 'the sense', is lost. It is similar to the rewinding of a film or video tape where the sense or the meaning then become divorced from the original context.

## Analysing the results

The first tentative implication of this study is that information concerning cognitive development appears in movement, where children use their bodies as a major framework of reference, before other more established contexts. This discovery signals an important, additional dimension to the movement component of early childhood education and care. Since this piece of research was carried out (1976) the notion of a fixed and developmental order in the acquisition of logical operations has been challenged and accordingly modified. The important issue now is to examine relevant notions of movement-related cognition in the light of current educational theory.

Immediately following the completion of the research study the children were asked to paint about their climbing, balancing and jumping activities. It was found that degrees in accurate and detailed verbal description, which was already shown to correspond to the detail and complexity of their movement activity, in turn tied up with the children's ability to represent their three actions pictorially. It is interesting to see the way the children have 'composed' their paintings to give the picture 'as they see it'. Matthews (1994) draws attention to the important role that composition plays in young children's paintings and makes the point that it is not an optional affair.

### Mandy's painting

Mandy's painting (figure 32) shows a clear differentiation of activity. The act of jumping is indicated by the space she has left between the two boxes and, although balancing does not show her feet in contact with the bench, the outstretched arms give important information about what is going on. Climbing is less immediately distinguishable, although there is some indication of the vertical uprights of the climbing frame and, therefore, the up-up-down direction in which the activity takes place.

### Luke's painting

Luke's painting (figure 33) shows much clearer representation. The action of balancing indicates both feet in contact with the bench and arms are helping too. In the representation of jumping we see that the body is clearly in front of the box over which the leap has taken place. There can be no doubt that this is Luke's favourite activity. Climbing, again proving to be the most difficult action to convey, is communicated partly through the vertical and horizontal structure of the climbing frame.

### Alison's painting

Alison's painting (figure 34 on page 56) shows a similar representation to Luke's. Outstretched arms and firmly planted, 'footless legs', indicate balancing while a space between the 'footless legs' and bench clearly indicate jumping. It is interesting to note the absence of arms in this action which could be interpreted as being less important and, by their very omission here, emphasise the use of them in balancing. Climbing is well expressed in the case of the frame but places the body in front of it.

The next two paintings resemble more closely the activities as they were executed. The 'sophistication' in comparison with the three previous paintings is clear.

*Figure 32    Mandy's painting*

*Figure 33    Luke's painting*

*Figure 34    Alison's painting*

### Joanna's painting

In contrast to the paintings of the five-year-olds, all three activities in Joanna's painting show the body facing a different, and appropriate, direction (figure 35). The use of hands and feet, more detailed here, all show relevance; we see her 'pushing off' the stool in jumping, 'attached to' the bench in balancing, and 'gripping' the rope in climbing. The articulated knee joints are also worthy of note and add to the 'movement feel'. It is interesting to speculate at this stage of 'visual realism' whether experiential activity – that is, carrying out the activities themselves – together with more highly developed observational skills may have helped towards the clarity seen in this painting.

### Mark's painting

The experiential probability is especially relevant to Mark's painting (figure 36). For example, the use of the arms is differentiated in some detail. The regulatory, two-dimensional position gives an impression of striving to maintain balance while the more mobile expression of the arms suggests flight of a more fluid nature. There is an expression of feeling in this painting which is referred to by Ives as 'content expression' (1984, Vol. 54, pp. 152–159). With the hair standing on end, and the implied height of the jump through its placement in relation to the other activities in the picture, we are led to believe that this is an exciting

*Figure 35    Joanna's painting*

*Figure 36    Mark's painting*

experience. While climbing is shown in a rather static, symmetrical pose, distance and perspective are all in evidence and, unlike the paintings of the five-year-olds, the body is shown facing the 'well remembered' design of the climbing frame.

## On to the next stage

Some interesting information arises from this research, and associated studies, in terms of stages of cognitive development and links with movement. However, what is most needed now is information which relates to specific movement activities and the schematic development of these in early childhood learning. There are several research studies about the ways in which 'academic concepts' can be taught through the medium of movement (Humphrey, 1965; Cratty, 1971; Kirchner, 1974; Miller et al, 1975; Gallahue et al, 1975) but, in this chapter, we are primarily concerned with the place and importance of movement as a common denominator of cognitive development, and of ways in which children's thinking may be developed.

# MOVEMENT AND SPATIAL EMPHASIS

The number and refinement of interdependent actions which children possess at any given time is reflected, in part, in the spatial use of their bodies within the environment in which they move.

Gerhardt (1973) is almost exclusively concerned with ways in which young boys and girls orientate themselves in space. Through her many detailed examples she shows how body movement is recognised as an underlying and essential component of children's learning. She writes (p. 12):

> *Body movement is the foundation of thought. It derives from, and contributes to, sensory perception, imagery and thought. Each human being organizes his experiences into his own patterns.*

When young children balance along walls, climb over gates, jump over streams and activate see-saws they are developing notions of space. Through these, and a variety of associated actions, they come to know about such things as height, width, distance and proximity. Spatial knowledge which comes about when children respond to the environment in this active way, is an important part of learning and a good one to start with here.

## Observing Kriss at play

The following activities were observed in a play area for young children over a period of twenty minutes.

Three-year-old Kriss was one of many children enjoying the facilities in his local park. He was well co-ordinated and rhythmical in his movement and extremely agile in the activities he carried out. However, on this particular occasion, observation was mainly directed to the spatial use of his body and the consequent learning which was taking place. Although the level of Kriss' activity was intense it was restricted mainly to two situations, to which he kept returning. His spatial concentration seemed focused on three components, namely, 'up', 'down' and 'through'.

Climbing up the scrambling net and sliding down the pole was an activity repeated time and time again, always with a pause at the top platform before making his descent. 'I'm a fireman' he said, 'they have to get there quickly'. On all counts it was clear that Kriss climbed up in order to slide down – the favourite part of his activity (figure 38).

Kriss found one other situation in which to make a sliding descent when he chose to use the ladder and adjoining chute. This activity he also repeated many times. The passage to his starting place at the bottom of the ladder was often obstructed by other children and, at first, rather than take an alternative and sometimes shorter route, he stuck to his original circuit in spite of the obstructions he met and the time it took to get there. Having climbed the ladder he sometimes found the entrance to the chute already in use and had to wait his turn. On such occasions, although he couldn't see the person waiting for him at the bottom of the chute, because other children were having their turn, he called out 'Wait for me, I'm coming' (figure 39).

In addition to the up-down dimension, the two alternating activities which Kriss pursued have two other things in common. One is the climbing action and the other, more significant here, is the type of descent. In both instances this involved a sensation element of the body being 'taken over' by the movement in response to its own weight. However, within this similarity there were two significant differences. Once positioned at the top of the chute, the release of the hands was all that was needed to set his body in motion for the downward journey. In addition to the sense of exhilaration this was, in fact, less demanding in terms of physical exertion than the 'fireman's slide' where the hands had to grip the pole. Another glance at the photograph of Kriss coming down the pole shows that, at this stage, he does not use his feet in order to take some of the weight of his body although there is some attempt to position them

Figure 37    Symmetrical position adopted while climbing

Figure 38    'Being a fireman' sliding down the pole

Figure 39    Waiting for a turn – out of sight

appropriately. The considerable bodily demands in using the pole in this way may have had something to do with the pause Kriss made at the top each time as if preparing himself for the descent. They may also have prompted the periodic change Kriss made from this activity to the other.

Although there were two conventional slides in the play area Kriss did not choose to go on either of these although they were sometimes free. This may have been because the second spatial differentiation, prominent in his exploratory play, was 'going through' and, therefore, the chute which is enclosed like a tunnel was more relevant to this spatial schema than the slides which were open-sided and open-topped. On one occasion when his selection of 'going through' spaces were completely occupied Kris called 'I know, I know where I can go' and proceeded to leave the play area and run to an adjacent field where a stile led from one side to the other. Here, using the step which connected the two sides to squeeze himself 'through the gap', he proudly demonstrated his new activity.

Kriss was verbalising to himself as he went along, and, at intervals, he also verbalised his actions to his father and his friends. His language was almost entirely related to what he was doing in terms of action, with frequent references to his body and where movement was happening in terms of its location. 'Words preserve actions through time. They label and thus generate experience.' (Gerhardt, 1973, p. 31).

From this twenty-minute movement exploration, which included many separate, spatially-oriented activities often experienced by young children in similar settings, we turn to three specific examples of moving and knowing.

## Over and under and round about

The first example of a child thinking through movement while exploring a stable environment is provided by Nicola, aged three years, who discovered an empty clothes rail while her aunt was paying her bill in a department store. It was an ordinary, orthodox kind of rail with lower and upper horizontal bars between two quite sturdy uprights. Nicola had established an activity around the bottom rail and one of the uprights, saying aloud this sequence to herself as she moved:

*under and over*
*under and over*
*under and over*
*round and round and round and round*

Both the activity itself, and the words she used to describe it, clearly establish this as a spatially – emphasised activity. However, as well as doing and verbalising, or rather as a result of it, Nicola had established an interesting rhythmic build-up with a decisive and impactive ending to the phrase. (See pp. 28–9 for an earlier reference to impulsive and impactive phrasing in early childhood.)

Unusual though this activity might appear within a fairly busy department store, for Nicola it was a normal response to investigate what was immediately at hand. Having confirmed that no-one was being inconvenienced or disturbed, the fact that her aunt allowed it to happen, along with her lack of anxiety, made for a stress-free shopping expedition. Nicola's happy engagement in the making and subsequent repetition of her new acitivity supports the notion put forward by Singer and Singer (1990, p. 63) that 'when children are able to play openly and freely they become good learners, developing their cognitive skills through the stepping stones of play'.

## It's me that makes it happen

The second example of children thinking through movement comes from a supermarket where, inside the store, two children waited with their parents to be let into the shopping area. The girl, aged about three, was experimenting with how near to the electronically-controlled gate she had to go in order for it to open. With the encouragement of her brother, aged about eight years, to 'go a bit further', or 'get nearer to the gate' she gradually became aware of the exact spot she needed to reach in order to activate it. Her squeals of delight were shared by her parents and the quite lengthy queue which had formed. While welcoming her success, the now completely involved onlookers were willing her to reach the next stage which was to understand that the gate would not close, thus allowing her to 'play the game' again, until she took herself away from the point of activation. The co-operation of her brother, this time through physical contact as he guided her away from where she stood, helped her to make this happen but it was clear from her expression that the success in this instance lacked the essential understanding on her part. Nevertheless, she continued to explore just how far she had to advance or retreat to cause the right response. With or without her brother's help – and always with support and shared delight from all around – it was fun. Both this activity, and that of Nicola's, gives information on how society values its children, and illustrates well many of the common principles identified by Bruce (1987, p. 10).

## Jumping and landing – a height and depth of experience

The following example also demonstrates an appropriateness of action in relation to a stable environment but is much more complex in nature. Although the spatial connotations are restricted to directions of up and down, the way in which these are extended and the deliberateness of the activity indicate a higher level of cognitive functioning.

A small group of four-, five- and six-year-old boys were jumping off a plank which was slotted into a climbing frame situated in the grounds of their school. After they had enjoyed this activity of jumping at the set height (which continued for some considerable time) they took out the plank and inserted it one section higher. This happened several times and, as the plank went up in height, and the boys had to climb further to reach it, there were different reactions. Some continued to jump confidently from the newly established positions, some dropped out immediately knowing from experience that they had reached their 'personal best' while one or two walked to the end of the plank and decided at the last moment whether or not to take off. In making a last-minute decision one boy expressed his deliberations in words. He said 'It's higher now, it's too high to jump, there's further to drop'.

Through a successive sequence of events this five-year-old had established a reference framework of jumping and landing. He connected the fact that he was 'higher' with having climbed up 'further' and having 'further' to drop. As part of this thought process he might also have been remembering the increasing lack of comfort, which accompanied each successive landing. It was this framework of experience, including feelings of pleasure and wariness, which became his guide to decision-making. It is interesting to note that although the climbing/jumping activity was essentially an individual one the children were, for the most part, working co-operatively alongside each other, involved in each other's efforts, watching and waiting upon events. Their behaviour characterised what Piaget calls 'the stage of incipient co-operation'.

In essence, the children involved in this activity were constructing their own knowledge through a series of self-set challenges incorporating spatial notions, identified in Chapter 1 (pp. 15–18):

- direction: up and down;

- extension and size: big and little and near and far;

- zones: above and below;

- levels: high and low.

Although all these aspects of space were incorporated into the children's activity it is interesting to note that one theme, namely levels, incorporating high and low, was dominant with extension, size and direction being implied rather than emphasised. It is clear that different children were at varying stages of this wide and complex area of cognitive functioning. On the whole the younger children concentrated on one or two things at a time, whilst the older ones showed what Piaget describes as operational thinking. The boy who was considering whether to jump or not was obviously able to reflect upon his experience to date, and to make a decision in the light of it.

## Seriation: seeing the differences between things

In addition to cognitive recognition of space there are clear indications in the boy's jumping activity of the concept of seriation. Seriation is about seeing the difference between things and in respect of this and classification (seeing similarities), Athey (1990, p. 41) writes:

> *Seriation and classification have their origins in early actions applied to a wide range of objects and, later, to events. The common-sense world contains sufficient information to feed seriation structures such as size, height, weight, strength, temperature, porosity, number and so on.*

It is interesting to note that the first two seriation structures Athey lists, namely size and height, have a place in the space section of the movement classification (pp. 15–18). Also that her reference to strength relates to the dynamic notion of weight (pp. 11–12). As the group of boys were actively engaged in their jumping 'event' they could be said to be seriating their movement in the following ways:

- by positioning the plank increasingly higher up the frame;

- by climbing higher at each turn;

- by looking down from increasing heights;

- by jumping from increasing heights.

Significantly, all these seriation components are associated with the children's major focus on level ranging from high to low. The notion of high to low in this case was a personal as well as general notion – one boy's highest was different from that of another's. A further example of the decreasing number of children 'left in' also has a seriation slant but this did not feature prominently until towards the end when only one or two boys were 'still in'.

We will return to children's ordering of movement activities later in this chapter but, meanwhile, look at other activities showing how children learn through movement.

## Handling small games equipment

Children learn in particular ways when they explore and challenge features of their natural and man-made environment. We have just looked at some of these. The learning experience is of a different kind when they handle objects and make them move at will. Finding out 'what I can do' with a particular object is a lengthy and absorbing area of behaviour which stretches from the explorations of babies right through to the professional games player. Children employ a range of basic actions in order to make objects move and to keep them moving. These include:

- rolling;
- sliding;
- throwing;
- catching;
- striking;
- propelling.

Knowing 'how' to carry out these activities involves the 'thinking body' in dynamic action, making on-the-spot estimations based on lengthy periods of trying things out; of relating to elements of weight, size, shape and the movement properties of different pieces of apparatus.

### Self-made rules
Little has been said, so far, about the rules which govern games activity. In the first instance, rules are self imposed boundaries that children place on their play and which, perhaps, they do not even regard as rules. The demand of a young child to 'Watch me, you see I have to stand behind this line and then throw it' is an example of such self-made regulations. No-one suggested to the child that he or she had to stand behind the line. Often young children play their games in the same area as other children. This is either because a special time is set for the activity or because individual children join in with the activities of those

around them. Sometimes they share an idea. But only rarely, before the age of three, do they 'share each other'. All the same, as they bowl their hoops or kick their balls they acquire a sense of other children taking part and being involved.

As children tip over into a more co-operative period they play at first with one other, gradually extending into small groups. Their own skill and love of activity remain dominant features; their association with the other children is flexible and subsidiary and only a few rules bind them together. These rules are, at first, changeable and loose, arising from the restrictions and opportunities momentarily encountered. Coats substituting as goal-posts, lines on the pavement indicating areas of play and conveniently placed trees denoting boundaries, all have a part to play in regulating 'the game'. So too do the procedures which govern their play. Times for changing over and taking on other roles, along with notions of supremacy, are mutually agreed. Because the rules and regulations are the children's own they understand them even if the adults to whom they are explained may have some initial difficulty!

Sometimes, play is coloured by images from the professional world. For example, a common sight in football-type games, played by children as young as five and six, is the almost horizontal launch of the goal-keeper saving a goal which is sometimes in no need of saving! As it happens so often, and with such conviction, this seemingly compulsive action must have a lovely bodily feel, as well as perhaps a sense of 'saving the day'. In tune with the professional scene, the scoring of goals is often accompanied by cheers and hugs all round. The games play of five- and six-year-olds shows other ways in which external models are there *in situ* but not necessarily integrated. Sometimes the children set up two goal areas and have two groups acting as teams. Often both teams play co-operatively and into one goal! At half-time, a time of their choosing, *all* players change over and play towards the other goal. The goal-keeper, if there is one, simply goes to the other goal area which, until this moment, has remained unused.

As games develop in skill and strategies, and children make a transition into competitive games, so their involvement in the rules and regulations which govern their games increases. It is well known that at the top of the junior school such detail often hampers the actual playing of the game itself. On the other hand it is a time when umpiring and reporting skills begin to take their place along with those of performance.

## Looking at the apparatus

Some of the games-like equipment which we provide for children at home and in nursery settings share common properties. For example, they can be made to travel along the ground and through the air in a variety of directions and with different degrees of force. However, individual pieces of equipment – balls, bean bags, hoops, quoits, bats, sticks – have special identity features of their own. At one time it was thought that a young child's selection of small apparatus was a random affair. We know now that this is unlikely to be the case and that children are continually searching for materials and experiences which will 'feed' their current stock of schemas (Athey, 1990, p. 41). Examples of such feeding, that is the identification of movement-associated schemas, and appropriate provision to develop them, would take a longer time than this chapter permits. Therefore, just a few references to one piece of equipment, namely hoops, are included to suggest how this might be done.

## Using hoops in play

Some of the special features of a hoop can be classified in this way:

- its circularity is continuous and enclosed;

- it remains the same shape whether it is lying on the floor, hanging on a storage peg or being held in the hand;

- it has an inside which is enclosed and space which surrounds it;

- it can surround and enclose the body, parts of the body and other objects;

- it can be rolled;

- it can be spun.

At first hoops are used without any reference to their special properties. In common with any other objects feeding their 'transporting' schema, very young children may simply carry them from place to place. Whalley (1994, pp. 93–94) gives examples of ways transportation schema can be extended for the under-fives. Marcus, aged two, was one of a group of children aged between two and eleven who were playing together. He carried his hoop around while watching the older children use theirs in a variety of different ways. Anxious to join in, it was at this moment that Marcus put his head through his hoop (see figure 40 on page 68).

Eventually, children use hoops in relation to their specific features, the stage they have reached in their personal 'handling skills' and their own movement appetite. They send them rolling and spin them on the ground, round their

*Figure 40    Being enclosed*

waists, arms and legs. They use them to jump into, out of and over. Later they become goals and target areas in solitary, co-operative and competitive games situations. And at times they become racing cars, parachutes and traffic roundabouts as children engage in their symbolic play.

## Family games: mother and daughter

Learning through movement goes on everywhere and not least of all in the home. In figures 41, 42 and 43 we can see that three-year-old Harriet is experiencing a great deal of movement activity which carries spatial connotations. She is finding out that her body can do exciting, agile things. Expertly supported, and feet first, she goes up, over and down again – a backward somersault in the air. For the whole of the acrobatic journey she is passing through her mother's arms.

This, and similar agility activities, may happen very quickly in which case the continuity and flow are all-important. On other occasions, selected parts of the game can occur more slowly in order to emphasise what is taking place. Accompanying words from the mother such as 'Up you go', 'Over you go' and 'Down you come' will help to register the spatial significance of the various parts of the activity as they occur – words in which the children can also join.

*Figure 41    Up*
*Photo © Catherine Ashmore*

*Figure 42    Over*
*Photo © Catherine Ashmore*

*Figure 43    And down*
*Photo © Catherine Ashmore*

This shared activity illustrates well the relationship category of movement first referred to on page 23. While the mother's role is appropriately dynamically supportive Harriet is doing her bit too. She is working hard in terms of energy and her body is very active. Notice how her feet lead the way and how well placed they are. Her head goes backwards as her mother gently tips her to start her on her downward path. Harriet is obviously confident in this companionable play situation and her expression is one of fluency and ease. There needs to be mutual trust in movement activity of this sort as well as understanding of how to hold and to help.

## Family games: brothers play together

Two brothers, Martin, aged eight and Graham, aged six, had set up a game for themselves, along the lines of cricket. All aspects of the game were related to what was available in terms of resources and their individual understanding at that time. In determining the length of the pitch it was agreed that they would measure this by a given number of strides. In terms of assessing how many of his strides would approximate to a reasonably accurate distance Martin took the lead here and began measuring the pitch. But perceiving the situation from his point of view Graham warned him, saying, 'Not big steps because I can't bowl that far'. Implicit in this comment was Graham's ability to relate Martin's length of stride to the distance to the proposed wicket. This, in turn, related to his own ability in bowling which was different from his brother's.

## The ordering of events – seriation

Seriation – seeing the differences between things – is usually attributed to the stage of operational thought starting around the age of six years although, as we saw in the boys' climbing and jumping activities on pages 63–4, comprehension can emerge earlier. There are many movement-oriented examples of ways in which children order in a relational way along the lines that each successive 'move' is less, or more, than the preceding one. They are much in evidence in the junior school playground in such games as 'Donkey', 'Sevens', leap-frogging over an increasing number of backs, decreasing the space through which a ball has to be thrown, and running and leaping to touch a spot higher than the one before. 'Adding to' and 'taking away' from are central to such instances of movement play, and ways in which these ideas are fed from a variety of movement content will continue to be considered within the learning/teaching context in Chapter 4.

# Making things more difficult; a challenge and fun

The remarkable amount of self-initiated interests in 'ordering activities' often means going that bit further or finding another way of doing something. From an early stage children's movement activity is full of 'I can make what I am doing more difficult'. Later on, the challenge of 'I can do better than you' comes about. Competing to see who can put the most claps in between throwing a ball in the air and catching it is a simple example of what is meant here. To begin with, a whole group of children may take part in the contest without bothering to check who has won. This develops to a time when one or more children are intent on getting the better of the others – to be 'the best'.

Two seven-year-old friends, Nasreen and Shanaz, incorporated the notion of difficulty into their activity. They made up a throwing and catching game in which the object was to throw the ball from one to the other with a penalty imposed every time it was dropped. The penalty scale which they agreed upon, and which rendered a player increasingly less effective, was along the following lines:

- one hand only to catch;

- kneeling on one knee;

- kneeling on two knees;

- sitting down;

- out.

If, while in one of these 'penalty positions', the ball was successfully caught the player was allowed to return to the previous, more advantageous stage. In this way the players regained a hierarchical 'status' in the reverse order of its loss. This game is a clear example of a traditional one which was modified to meet Shanaz and Nasreen's needs.

Competition of this kind has to do with increasing skill and maturity and may relate to self-imposed goals, those traditionally handed down or a mixture of the two. Hierarchical variation in skipping is another example of increasing difficulty characterising competition with self and with others. The variations might be as follows:

- skipping forwards and backwards;

- crossing the rope in front and behind;

- 'doubles';

- skipping with a partner starting inside the rope;

- skipping with a partner, running in;

- skipping inside someone else's rope;

- running in, skipping in someone's rope and running out.

## Learning through dance

As a final example of children learning through movement we turn now to dance; and specifically to the bonfire dance of a group of six- and seven-year-olds. At a certain point in the dance they had to work out how to arrive in a group – the central bonfire – coming from positions around the edge of the hall. Sometimes it worked well. Sometimes it was a muddle. It was never the same twice. It was difficult for some of the children to think ahead and imagine how others were solving the problems of contributing to the group shape. A decrease in ego-centricity is characteristic of intellectual development in children between the approximate ages of six and eight. However, this increasing ability to give, take and put themselves in the position of other children (in this case literally) needs practice in situations such as this. Help from the teacher can be useful in establishing some anchor points of first arrivals and then encouraging the others to find a place, perhaps joining at once, or waiting until a space becomes free.

# SUMMARY

Some of the ways children learn through movement have been looked at both in general terms and through detailed analysis of specific activities. The next chapter makes use of these observations as it considers a variety of learning and teaching environments appropriate to the movement education of early childhood.

# 4 THE LEARNING AND TEACHING ENVIRONMENT

## MAKING A GOOD START

The importance of the right kind of environment is an early consideration of parents even before birth takes place. An over-abundance of literature and advice on such alternatives as home births, hospital births, water births, births to music, with or without fathers being present, is available to guide decision-making at this important time. From birth onwards young babies make sense of their environment through what they see, hear, touch, smell and their sense of movement.

Right from the start of life, physical activity and childhood seem natural partners (Shephard, 1982, p. ix). Innate stages of growth and maturation come and go with nods of approval and sighs of relief on the part of those concerned, as one landmark after another is noted. However, developing behaviour requires contributions from both the child and the environment (Katz, 1984, p. 31). The environment includes the all-important one of people: family and friends, either knowingly or intuitively, can be seen to 'feed' these stages with appropriate materials and experiences and so, to some degree, aid the process of development. For example, reaching and grasping, an early reflex action, is responded to by parents who, when carefully inserting a finger into the palm of the baby's hand feel the tightening of their grip with pride (Roberts and Tamburrini, p. 62).

Around the age of four months, purpose and intention replace the reflex grasping action and, with increasing eye-hand co-ordination, babies are able pick up objects, though less able to release them. At this stage of development environmental provision is made, in part, through a range of toys of appropriate size and weight provided by family and friends who, through their careful selection, take on an early teaching role. This role continues as interests and preoccupations change. With the approach of each birthday questions such as 'What is he into now?' or 'What does she like doing?' reflect wishes to support and strengthen the stage of functioning a particular child has reached.

The interaction of the environment with stages of growth and maturation throughout the first eight years of life is the nub of the educational process, a process which goes on at home and in all types of care and educational settings. All situations in which children learn are important and therefore it is vital that environmental provision is in position, and carefully considered, in every one of these.

A range of restraints such as geography, topography and climate inevitably limit a child's experience of physical pursuits (McPherson et al, 1989). However, although there are differences between families or home units, reflecting cultural, social and economic concerns, it would seem that most families are intent, right from the start, on providing as rich and supportive an environment as possible in order to extend spontaneous behaviour. The increasing use of specialised outlets such as Early Learning Centres, television programmes, play groups, library projects and many other similarly designed initiatives, all testify to the high regard with which the majority of families hold opportunities for education and the associated 'good start in life'. In support of this prevailing attitude Gillian Pugh and Erica De'Ath (1984, p. 169) write:

> *The great majority of parents are concerned to do their best for their children even if they are not always sure what this might be.*

However, as Boorman (1987, p. 233) suggests, it is often the case that only cognitive or intellectual development is considered important and the physical aspect of a child's development is disregarded or left to chance. In the light of the assumption identified earlier, that growth and hierarchical physical development appear to be pre-determined unless something occurs to interrupt or slow down the programme of events, this assessment of prevailing educational values is not difficult to understand. While some families sense that some provision is necessary, a good number think of provision in terms of allowing their children to be physically active, to let off steam, and to keep fit. All these are commendable justifications and it would be foolish to deny the importance of aims associated with a sense of well-being, physical fitness and confidence. All children deserve the opportunity to become self-assured and competent in controlling their moving bodies (Blenkin and Kelly, 1987, p. 231). But this is only part of the picture.

## LEARNING AND TEACHING: A MOVEMENT-BASED ENVIRONMENT

The learning and teaching environment can be related to specific categories of movement provision and to the stage of development reached by individuals and groups. As indicated in earlier chapters, children will always find ways to explore their immediate environment. For example, we saw the two-year-old with her push-chair and Nicola's exploration of the clothes rail. Both these children demonstrate the need of all children to do just that – explore the

*Figure 44    Bound flow accompanies new and difficult actions*

*Figure 45    A new environmental challenge*

immediate environment in which they find themselves. They also serve as examples of one particular movement appetite as do those of Lucy, aged three, and Daniel, aged six, in figures 44 and 45 on page 75, who continue to respond to the challenges which the stable features of the physical environment offer.

These self-initiated activities need to be taken into account when making informed and imaginative provision of a general kind such as that suggested by Bruce (1987, p. 55):

> *Material provision makes the bones of the environment. It gives children first-hand experiences. It needs to be wide ranging, both indoor and outdoor with natural and manufactured objects. . . Simply providing sand, climbing frame, and a butterfly garden does not mean that children will learn about mathematics, movement or natural science.*

# THE HOME ENVIRONMENT

## An agility-friendly environment

Many families with access to gardens initially cater for their children through the provision of such equipment as climbing frames, swings, see-saws, clambering blocks, large blocks and tree houses. For those homes in the form of flats, bed and breakfast accommodation, or houses without space around them, play in proximity to home still features prominently. Pedestrian walkways, 'no traffic' streets and reserved play spaces on housing estates all give regular access to railings, steps, walls and gates to stimulate agile activity. The immediacy and regularity of opportunity and experience which the local neighbourhood, like the garden, provides is enticing and many children do, indeed, play in local haunts. If the immediacy and regularity of garden and street play are advantages, then the drawback lies in their unalterability and this is where trips to parks, commons and adventure playgrounds are all-important.

Agility in the water is equally valued as part of early childhood provision. Water skills and swimming are life skills which should be introduced as early as possible. The enjoyment of fun bath times, garden paddling pools and visits to the children's pools at the local baths all combine to make children water-confident and secure.

Whenever possible, home-based agility apparatus should reflect the changing stages of development of the children using it – not an easy task if the home unit contains two or more children below eight years of age. Increasingly, knowledge about ways in which children learn have informed the design of agility equipment. Equipment which differs in size and proportions is an important consideration as well as equipment which can be changed and modified in some way, by children and adults, as illustrated by the boys who changed the level of the plank in their jumping activity on pages 63–5. The in-built design features of the majority of garden apparatus mainly defy change, which means that increased skill and versatility have to come from the children's own bodily versatility rather than their response to the structures themselves. Examples of this include missing out alternative rungs when climbing to the top of the frame; coming down without using the feet, using the swing while standing, or jumping off it when it is still moving.

As suggested earlier, skilled movement in a safe and dependable setting, such as the garden or immediate neighbourhood, needs to be experienced elsewhere in an extended and less predictable context. All young members of the family can be catered for in outings to parks, adventure playgrounds or the countryside where a three-year-old may seek places to try out his/her balancing, a five-year-old will find stones and rocks where he/she can jump from and an eight-year-old will climb and jump from trees. All these activities will reflect the interest or craze of the moment.

## All I need is me – and sometimes you

Bodily agility without reference to structured apparatus is, in some ways, simpler to provide for and certainly less expensive. This is the time when children concentrate on their bodies alone. They spend a great amount of time finding out what their bodies will do – and will not do. Obviously, the garden, the approaches to the house and flexible interiors are important here, and even more so if they incorporate grass, paved areas, slopes, steps, carpets and cushions; places where children can stand on their hands and their heads, run, roll and balance as they work towards their acrobatic and athletic potential.

As children respond readily to this type of environment in which they regularly find themselves, tests of inventiveness and skill are developed in response to their own bodies as well as to 'models' passed on by, and shared with, family and friends. It is interesting to observe how skilfulness gives way to set skills. Children discover the right time to stop or continue; they are able to judge their own moments of personal readiness, for example, looking between their legs and performing all sorts of tumbling activities before embarking on a forward somersault. David, aged four, is seen in figure 46 on page 78 trying out what it is like to be nearly upside down. Or perhaps he wants to do a forward roll. He has three points of contact with the floor – the head and two hands.

*Figure 46    Three points of balance*

Outings to parks and open spaces are equally important for acrobatically and athletically stressed activities where landscaping featuring banks, slopes, hills, trees, gullies, stepping stones and river banks provide a more extensive range of opportunities than can be experienced at home.

'Significant other people' (Bruce, 1987, p. 107) feature prominently in this area of movement; a hand to steady legs in first attempts to balance upside down, to help the head tuck in as a forward roll is begun, to hold the stick to be jumped over, and to join in the race – although not necessarily to win!

## Where games begin

Here the important aim is to provide an environment to develop children's dexterity and, primarily, their attempts to make objects move or to deal with those already moving. Wetton (1988, p. 111) calls these 'manipulative skills'. As indicated earlier, this is a complex operation where attention has to be given to both the body and the object being rolled, thrown, caught, struck or propelled in some other way. Although interest in games-like activities exists from an early age, development is less marked than in some other areas of activity and involves elements of unpredictability and change. A tree to be climbed is relatively static, providing a consistency of experience. On the other hand, bouncing a ball, which when mastered seems such a simple activity, is an example of a constantly changing operation often presenting five-year-olds with difficulties in perception and hand-eye co-ordination. It is a considerable challenge to combine agility, athletic prowess and manipulative skill in activities of this kind. The complexity of such operations makes it clear why young children have to concentrate so intently, why there is such a constant need to practise and why there is such a diversity of attainment in this area of movement. In figure 47, Richard, who is six, shows how far he has come in catching a ball. He is focusing well and his arms and hands are ready to receive it. Soon he will learn to step towards it so that he is in the right place. As he gains confidence from increased experience and success the bound flow restriction which characterises his stance will lessen, although he will need to keep hold of some of this in order to be precise and efficient.

In providing for experience in games-oriented activities, a range of types of equipment, as well as a variety of shapes, sizes, and colour, is important. Very young children need things which are soft and malleable to grasp in initial attempts to throw and catch and striking surfaces need to be wide. Reduction illustrates greater expertise on the part of the handler, as does the manipulation of two pieces of apparatus.

*Figure 47    Early attempts at catching*

## Shall we dance?

Dance is arguably the least difficult area of provision to make at home and yet, perhaps because it seems less tangible than its counterparts, it is often the area least well catered for. In the absence of permanent external structures such as agility apparatus, bats and balls to occupy limbs or to direct focus, dance-like activity is most often only fleetingly glimpsed and not always registered.

While welcoming such transient moments of predominantly spontaneous activity, dance, like all other types of movement, needs to be woven into the daily routine. Above all children need space to dance which may entail pushing furniture to the walls, opening up communicating rooms or finding a quiet corner of the garden. Sound is sometimes helpful in getting children to dance. They might also be encouraged to put sounds to the dances they have already made. A store of musical instruments such as maracas, castanets, drums and gongs, as well as a few tapes of sound and music, are good to have at hand. Dressing-up clothes and 'props' play their part too; such things as cloaks, scarves, ribbons, clogs, hats and swords all bring a special 'feel' to children's dancing. Taking part alongside others is something young children enjoy and to be a partner who is held in the arms of an adult and 'danced' is a particular joy.

*Figure 48   Harriet and her mother dance together   Photo © Catherine Ashmore*

# MOVING AWAY FROM HOME

## Provision for the youngest children

Differences towards provision within nursery-type settings lie first and foremost in the justification for movement as part of the 'early childhood curriculum'. In this context the curriculum refers to elements which characterise a particular setting. These, in turn, reflect the current value system of that particular establishment. At home both the nature and extent of movement provision relate to personal decisions by the parents and to availability of space. It varies within and between home units, in regularity and content. Although no statutory provision exists, there appears to be common agreement that children below five years of age need to engage in physical activity. While the reasoning seems little different from that which prompts its inclusion in the home, the way in which movement is featured in early childhood settings is different in kind.

At present, movement is considered within a setting combining care and education and, as such, has aims and objectives related to its provision and implementation. In terms of resources, provision may not be dissimilar to that of the home setting but in most cases there will be more of it. The design of agility structures is likely to be more informed, and at its best, provides a common resource, both indoors and out, for all the children irrespective of previous provision. Children of this age need both stable and mobile equipment which use the large muscle groups. This equipment might include barrels and tyres they can crawl through, trucks and trolleys and a variety of wheeled toys they push, pull and pedal.

For the three children in figure 49 (page 82) their transport play was a rich learning situation. Increasing her passengers from one to two produced some initial difficulty for the 'driver' in making a start and in keeping going. 'It won't go' she said. The ensuing conversation about the reasons for this increased difficulty involved notions of energy on the part of the 'driver', who realised that she had to pedal much harder, weight, because it was more heavily loaded, and numbers, because there were two passengers instead of one. Although it was not verbalised in any way it was interesting to note that steering was also affected. No longer was 'cornering' included in the journeys which now consisted of straight pathways taken at a slow pace. Ideally, these children will now be encouraged to take part in similar situations in which they can compare weight, number, and energy output and come to further conclusions based on their own experiential observations.

*Figure 49    Sorting out energy, load and number*

The most important resource of all is the adults, professionally educated in matters of child development, who select equipment and materials, promote the most relevant form of learning experiences, and are on hand throughout the day to help give increased meaning to activities undertaken. Their calibre and training are key determinants of high quality provision (Ball, 1994, p. 56). This view is supported by Tamburrini (1982, p. 109) who comments:

> *A high level of expertise is required to educate young children within an informed curriculum where there is a synchrony between the children's intentions and the educational dialogues the teacher initiates.*

An important role of early childhood educators is to make the most of what each and every child has to offer when they join the nursery setting. Perhaps assessment of what this might be is easier to make in terms of movement than in certain other areas of experience – it is certainly as large as life! One such role, identified by Athey (1990, p. 41) and which continues as a major one throughout the whole of primary education, is to:

*feed spontaneous structures with content not necessarily found at home, street or playground. In other words, worthwhile curriculum content can be offered that, if received, will extend cognitive structures educationally. Within the highest concept of education, teaching 'fleshes out' spontaneous and natural concepts with worthwhile curriculum content.*

Given an overall acceptance that movement provision is an important constituent of early childhood, its nature and content relate to a variety of care and education issues in evidence at a time when rapid physical and intellectual development characterise the life of the children who attend.

## Provision in primary schools

Once in the first year of mainstream education, one of the major differences for the children is in the structure of the day. In most, but not all, school situations, particular areas of learning, now labelled the primary curriculum, have their set place and allotted time span. The attention given to the teaching of the children, and therefore their learning, is increasingly orientated to legal requirements. Movement provision made by the teacher is now more likely to be contained within lesson units and those units related to longer termly, or yearly, developmental programmes. These reflect, in part, the current philosophy of the National Curriculum. However, whatever shape the more formally-structured movement curriculum takes, the children should be able to participate in any of the seven separate areas of the movement curriculum (athletics, dance, games, gymnastics, outdoor and adventurous activities and swimming) as these have their roots in the movement activities of early childhood. It is encouraging for early childhood educators to know that if children have been given appropriate provision, support and guidance in early movement activities at home, and in nursery settings, until at least the age of five years, problems in making a transition to the lesson demands of the infant school should be minimal (Pascal, 1990).

# Learning situations: a flexible guide

Although ways in which learning and teaching strategies take place are different in the home, nursery, infant and junior school settings, there are certain phases of experience which are common to all of these. They are:

- free exploration;
- adult-led experiences;
- consolidation;
- extension.

These four phases can usefully serve as guidelines for all types of activity sessions and by children of all ages provided they are used flexibly and relevantly.

# Free exploration

Free exploration means exactly what it says and refers to children's untutored response to any movement-related situation in which they find themselves, whether this is in a cot, beside a stream, on a grassy slope or in a highly organised gymnastics or dance lesson. Free exploration allows children to move in any way they wish. It describes an open-ended, non-interventionist learning situation, and represents one end of a continuum which has, at its other end, the direct and detailed teaching of set skills. It occurs at times when, activated only by personal wishes and within safety limits provided by those responsible, children investigate the mobile and static environment in which they find themselves. Unfortunately, free exploration as a mode of movement experience was over-used in the 1960s, the age of child-centred education, and was consequently relegated by some writers to an initial and low-level stage of behaviour associated with 'the young, the timid and the unsure' (Churcher, 1971, p. 16). If exploration goes on for too long without guidance Churcher suggests that 'the work tends to revert in character to the "play" of the nursery stage'. The general view of the physical educationalists of the 1960s was that fast on the heels of exploration follow different, more advanced strategies such as skill acquisition and problem-solving. The implication of this was interpreted by some to mean that problems are not solved through exploration, skill is not acquired through exploration and that people cease to explore after they are young, timid or unsure. In fact free exploration can be seen to apply to all stages of movement education and recreative pursuits and the views expressed here are in agreement with Hutt (1966) who sees it as a serious and concentrated activity.

## Schemas and free exploration

The wide-ranging set of movement possibilities seen in terms of the body, space, dynamics and relationships, as set out in Chapter 1, could be re-classified as a repertoire of 'schemas'.

Children arriving at nursery school have at their disposal a number of actions such as running, jumping, balancing, gesturing, twirling and climbing, and know about such things as being high up and low down, stretched out and curled up, and moving slowly and quickly. Free exploration of a new environment allows these bodily, dynamic and spatial schemas to be used to their full. The children have the ability to 'deal with an environmental event in terms of his current structures' (Ginsburg and Opper, 1969, p. 18) or, as Athey, writing more recently, suggests, 'Experience is [thus] assimilated to cognitive structures and this is how knowledge is acquired' (1990, p. 37). The intensity with which children use a currently compelling schema cannot be mistaken; they may climb the scrambling net repeatedly, constantly twirl round and round, pedal a tricycle tirelessly up and down the path or come down the slide time and time again. A similar intensity may be seen in the 'intertwining' activities of an eight-year-old as she tries out her bodily mobility on the agility frame or dribbles a ball up and down the football pitch.

## Extending Schemas

Sometimes children's schemas are 'opened out' a little and they become more generalised. For example, five-year-olds who have experienced balancing along the library wall, the high kerbstone outside the school or in other varying self-chosen locations may find that in the PE lesson there are two metal poles with a space in between as part of the agility apparatus. Faced with the prospect of balancing in this new situation they may be able to adapt their current action schema of balancing or, alternatively, may have to modify it in order to accommodate the unfamiliar structure. Modifying or accommodating behaviour of this kind was observed in the attempts of a seven-year-old girl, Tanya, who, adept at climbing fixed vertical ladders, met for the first time a rope ladder. Clearly, she was not prepared for several of the differences which she encountered:

- the mobile, swinging nature of the rope ladder;

- its fixture at one end only;

- the rope which replaced wood.

Equally clear, however, was the fact that, despite these significant differences, some features of the rope ladder were familiar to her. The horizontal rungs and the verticality of the ladder were the very things which, in the first instance, probably suggested to her that here was a place where she could fulfil her love of climbing. Only after a great deal of practice did she emerge equipped with an extended set of climbing-related schemas – and with increased self-confidence.

### Schemas become more co-ordinated

In arguing the case for periods of free exploration for learners of all ages it is important to stress that there should be some element present which makes the situation different for young children at home and in nursery settings from those attending infant and junior schools. As the process of assimilation continues through life the difference must lie within the schemas themselves. Like all schemas, movement schemas gradually become more co-ordinated and include a host of complicated ideas. An example at the simplest level might be the attempts of a five-year-old to swing on a rope. The agile way in which eight-year-olds can use one or two ropes to swing and climb illustrates a more advanced level, while at the far end of the spectrum is the trapeze artist who can swing using a variety of body parts for support and execute a series of stunts in the air. At the highest level of functioning we find choreographers composing from armchairs and olympic coaches making up routines for the parallel bars far from the sports hall. Action has become truly internalised into thought.

## Adult-led experiences

While acknowledging that through the nature of provision, and comments and suggestions made by adults, there is an element of in-built guidance in free exploration, its presence in adult-initiated exploration is more specific in terms of facilitating, shaping and influencing movement outcomes. Experiences which are adult-led refer to the channelling of movement responses through suggestions, tasks and challenges set by parents, teachers, and others involved. Used appropriately it is a phase of learning which, through degrees of limitation, brings about:

- greater versatility;

- increasing skilfulness;

- clarity of intent and outcome.

Adult-led experience varies greatly according to the context in which it is used. Usually the younger or more inexperienced the child is, the wider and more generalised the movement challenge. It is relatively easy to find appropriate challenges for individual children as they move at home or in nursery settings and to be able to pick up on what they have been recently doing. For example, suitable suggestions might be 'to find places to jump from the frame', 'to try out the things you were doing on the mat' or 'to dance to a favourite piece of music'. Sometimes, however, parents and teachers have to relate to a small group of children who are sharing a space or some equipment and then the suggestions made have to be general enough for each child to take up. Limitation of any kind demands some degree of accommodation on the part of individuals and the more specific and demanding the task the less likely everyone in the group or class will be able to comply. Challenges can be simple or complex and narrow or wide in design according to the amount of individual response envisaged. In the next chapter, suggestions for challenging children's movement invention and skill at varying stages of development will be listed but, at this point, it might be helpful to think of individuals or groups of children who would be able to cope with the following suggestions. To have particular children in mind, as these are read, helps to fit challenges to landmarks of learning.

- Make your hands and feet dance to the music.

- Stretch your body as much as you can while you move on the apparatus.

- Practise bouncing your ball at different heights as you run with it.

- Move on your hands and feet on the agility frame and travel in one direction only.

- Make up a dance which has three sections and end small and close to the ground.

As children's expertise grows and their movement schemas become increasingly complex and co-ordinated, so set patterns of movement begin to play a part in lessons as well as in outside clubs and organisations. Ballet and contemporary dance classes, skiing holidays, swimming, rambling and games clubs are just a few of the out-of-school activities which begin to command interest at this point.

## Consolidation

Children need time to consolidate and become secure in their recently acquired skills. As well as carrying out their activities in familiar contexts they need to reinforce them in situations of similar difficulty. There is sometimes a tendency on the part of parents, teachers, and others concerned, to build one layer of skilful or inventive activity on top of another – a hierarchically-structured pattern of learning – which sometimes results in stress as increasingly difficult challenges cannot be met by many children.

It is hard for adults not to encourage so-called advancement because they know only too well what might come next. We can recall the overtly expressed wish of some primary school children (perhaps, in part, expressing the anxiety of parents) to go on to the next, more complex book – because to do so implies progress and 'keeping up' – rather than to enjoy other books of a comparable standard and thus come to love the activity and reward of reading for pleasure and reading with ease. Such lateral experience, or sideways extension, essential to good practice in literacy, is equally important in movement education. It is important because, in this way, children are given opportunities to use their new movement knowledge and understanding, be it in dance, games, or gymnastics, in a variety of situations. And, not least, because it gives the current state of children's experience, the here and now, as much value as any anticipated, future goal. Margaret Donaldson (1932, p. 32) warned about the danger of 'acquiring language rather than learning to speak'. In similar vein, Keith Swanwick (1982, p. 9), referring specifically to arts education, argues that:

> Education is surely more than having 'experiences' or acquiring a repertoire of skills and facts. It has to do with developing understanding, insightfulness; qualities of mind.

Although Keith Swanwick's words refer to arts education they can be applied equally well to the whole of movement education. His message, and that of Margaret Donaldson, signify that the acquisition of the language of movement is not necessarily synonymous with learning to move.

In making a case for the inclusion of lateral experiences at each stage of development it should not be overlooked that, sometimes, children need to be encouraged to part company with movement activities with which they appear to be stuck and which have become rather meaningless. This may be a particular activity like rolling down the bank, a particular dance, or a favourite ball game. In all such situations adults will need to find ways for the children to 'move on', ways which, while respecting the familiar, will incorporate manageable units of unfamiliarity and thus ensure progression.

# Extension

This refers to a phase of activity where the aim is for children to enlarge and combine their movement schemas and thus become more versatile, skilful and 'personalised' in what they do. Children will perceive for themselves ways in which their activities can be extended. Readers will perhaps remember times from their own childhood when they went to bed hardly bearing to leave their current 'craze' and already thinking about what they were going to do with it the next day. However, in addition to free extension of this self-imposed sort, challenges set specifically for the children, and which are adult-led, play an increasingly important role, coming fully to fruition in the infant and junior school when adults become re-cast as teachers. Once again the complexity of demands needs to coincide with the current stage of functioning reached by individuals and groups of children. Which, in turn, implies that those involved in presenting those challenges need to be able to match them accurately.

## Matching

Children are the best 'matchers' in the world. They not only make good judges of what to do next but also of when to do it. Their ability here has some connection with the notion of 'seriated difficulty' which we looked at in detail earlier (p. 71), although versatility too plays an important part. Evidence of 'self-match' is plentiful as children volunteer what they are 'going to do next' or seek to show 'what they have just done'. Talking and assessing together at this juncture is an important part of learning and helps to consolidate what has taken place.

It is hard for teachers and parents to be as expert as their children in shaping progressive challenges which provide just the right amount of disturbance to their equilibrium, especially when dealing with groups or whole classes rather than individuals. But it is worthwhile persevering. The key to satisfactory matching, according to Willig (1990, p. 15), lies 'in finding challenging, but still manageable, learning experiences for children' which means estimating where they are functioning at any given time and then finding just the right potential extension for them to try out.

The lack of research and consequent dearth of sufficiently specific guidelines relating to the pitching of appropriate challenges is a severe disadvantage in movement education. Chris Athey (1990, p. 16) suggests that the greatest progress has been made in 'matching' what children can do with what children are offered in mathematics, science and language. On the other hand, there is an abundance of first-hand evidence of children's own do-it-yourself movement activity to guide us. The degree of struggle between what children can do and the demands of the next stage of achievement equates to the size of the gap between the two. The triumph of the 'I've done it' variety is seen in contrast to the anxiety and despondency shown when the discrepancy was too great, resulting in cries of 'I can't do it' or 'I give up'.

Even within these two extremes care must be taken to make sure we have 'gauged it right'. For example, in the first instance, the ability to solve the problem could be too immediate and effortless, demanding too small a leap while, in the second case, some additional help in the initial stages might make all the necessary difference to eventual success. Excessive praise might be as inappropriate a response in one situation as supporting the child's wish to give up in the other.

### Practice

Built into the children's ability to match up to movement challenges is the notion of practice which 'goes hand in hand with the development of know-how' (Arnold, 1979, p. 110). The kind of practising which takes place in relation to a set challenge is different from the passionate practising seen when young children use the apparatus at the start of a lesson (Brearley, 1969, p. 180).

If a challenge is the children's own, then so is their inner motivation and drive; through their practising they will be able to judge their own success or failure, to reach or fall short of their own inner models. At any time in the process they can change their model in response to how they view success or failure. For example, a seven-year-old may set himself the challenge of vaulting over an agility box, but, having tried this once or twice, without apparent success, he may change to jumping onto the box, travelling along it, and jumping off the other end – perhaps convincing himself that this was what was intended right from the start! A four-year-old, hesitating at the opening of the tunnel, may decide to run to the other end and look into it from there instead of making the expected journey through. However, this does not necessarily mean that attempts to carry out the original task cease. A variety of modifications and alterations may take place during subsequent tries and on the way to ultimate success. And with a perceptive adult at hand to help and encourage, that may not be too far ahead.

## SUMMARY: HALF AN HOUR WITH LUCY

This chapter is brought to an end with comments on a thirty-minute play period which Lucy, aged three ('four next Thursday'), shared with her mother. Lucy's play is seen in the context of a movement-based environment, the ways in which young children develop for themselves a skilled and versatile activity life, and how they interact with people. Learning/teaching phases of exploration, adult-led experiences, and consolidation and extension are looked at in the ways they relate to Lucy's activities. The role of Lucy's mother as she participates, looks and listens, sets the scene for the next chapter when the support, enrichment and extension of early movement activities are discussed.

On this occasion, Lucy's play environment consisted of a large, grassed area which sloped down to a straight, concrete path. Two sets of stone steps, each with a railing, plus two outsize rubber balls completed the scene.

Generally, the level of movement activity during the thirty-minute period was high. Lucy's action schemas included walking, running, balancing, jumping, galloping and turning. Although she changed freely from one to another throughout the afternoon, two schemas appeared to be more actively explored.

## Jumping

Lucy found all sorts of places to jump: she leapt onto the large rubber balls, into her mother's arms, and across the grass. At one point, using the path as a track, she made up a variety of jumping patterns, jumping from two feet to two feet, from one foot to the other, and from one foot to the same foot. From this personal collection Lucy persevered with her two-to-two jump, eventually 'accommodating' this to one of the two flights of steps. Starting at the fifth stair, she jumped down the steps one at a time (figure 50 on page 92) towards her mother who waited at the bottom ready to give her a high lift into the air to mark the end of the sequence. Lucy did this several times and it is interesting to note that, unlike Alexandra, who at an earlier stage tips herself off the steps into her father's arms (p. 31), Lucy was pushing off and achieving a 'real' jump. This was the first time Lucy had done this activity.

## Turning

Turning was the second of Lucy's action schemas which featured significantly in her play as she tumbled, half rolled, and turned round and round. She also experienced the sensation of turning in circles as her mother swung her round in a horizontal plane, parallel to the ground. Later on, when Lucy was once again tumbling and turning on the grass her mother asked 'Can you do this?' and quickly went into a cartwheel. Although the complexity of hand-foot co-ordination and the proximity of limbs for the purposes of weight bearing were

*Figure 50    Pushing off and coming down*

not within Lucy's comprehension, she immediately absorbed the circularity of the movement and managed a 'twisty turn'. This was another 'first' to add to her personal movement repertoire, and one which readily became one of her favourite activities to which she returned time and time again and which developed in understanding and skill throughout the afternoon. Later still, when she returned to the path on which she had originally tried out her jumping game, Lucy put her two most practised schemas, jumping and turning, together. Running along the path she took off and turned in the air. She was airborne for only a moment, and rose only a few inches from the ground but, nevertheless, as can be seen in Figure 51, it was indeed a turning jump.

*Figure 51    Turning and jumping: a co-ordinated schema*

## A new shape

One further discovery Lucy made during this intensive period of play was a new shape – a star shape where she became wide and stretched – which she can be seen sharing with her mother in figure 9 on page 9. Her delight in this newly-found activity was obvious and throughout the afternoon, and seemingly without any reason, she would take it up time and time again.

## Assessing Lucy's play

Lucy was involved in all four learning situations – exploration, adult-led experiences, consolidation and extension. Much of her initial and intermittent activity was exploratory where she made her own responses to the steps, railings, and grassy slopes of her immediate environment as well as to the acrobatic and athletic potential of her long and lean body. From time to time her mother led her into the second phase of learning by initiating activity through verbal suggestions or via her own activity. Where these were taken up the ideas were appropriately pursued, but when Lucy showed either disinterest, or dislike, the idea was immediately abandoned. In these instances Lucy usually took herself away for a short time and did something familiar and loved indicating that the distance between what she could do and what she was asked to do was too great. She could not accommodate to the new challenge. We have seen how Lucy involved herself in the third phase of consolidation when, for example, she tried out her separate jumping and turning in a variety of different, but similarly demanding, situations before going on to extend them. Eventually, her most complex co-ordination of the afternoon emerged when her action schema of turning was joined with her action schema of jumping to produce a turn in the air.

The way in which Lucy's mother was able to participate actively in Lucy's play was clearly a bonus in her learning experience. The dynamic, spatial images which she shared with her daughter through her bodily activity, and the excitement and pleasure she communicated on her own and Lucy's account, helped to make the experience an inviting and reassuring one.

The words which Lucy's mother used to identify, describe and expand her movements and the questions she asked, demanding both movement and verbal answers, also helped Lucy in her 'moving and knowing'. Whitehead (1990, p. 81) writes of the importance of children's language development in this way:

> A central concern of teachers should be to find ways of unlocking children's linguistic potential: stimulating a wider extension of active vocabulary resources and supporting more complex language performance.

In addition to practising current activities, and finding new ones, Lucy liked to recall earlier experiences. One of these was her 'floor dance' which she performed with the path as her stage (see Chapter 7) and at the end of which she gave a deep bow. There could be several reasons why this particular dance activity might have re-emerged as it did. In general terms, Lucy's mother is involved in dance education and therefore dance is a familiar activity. But, over and above that, Lucy was full of the fact that she was being taken to see *Coppelia* as a birthday treat. She could sing some of the music and remembered the story as it had been read to her a year or so previously.

Lucy's repetition and co-ordination of movement schemas throughout this period of activity has provided a fascinating study. It would be interesting now to continue these observations and record the next stage of development in Lucy's play along these lines for as Bruce (1987 p. 43) writes:

*The importance of the schema to the early childhood educator is that it provides a mechanism for analysing 'where the learner is' and helps predict analogous situations which will be of interest to the child.*

# 5 Supporting, Extending and Enriching Movement

## Selecting appropriate learning phases

In the previous chapter we saw that the phases of exploration, adult-led activities, consolidation and extension were selected not only because they relate easily to movement education as a specific area of learning, but also because they can be used flexibly in a variety of contexts from the earliest years at home to lessons in the junior school. Knowing what each phase represents, parents, family, friends, and early childhood educators can decide which ones are best suited to the children's current learning.

In the home, where one-to-one relationships often prevail, the sequence of phases will relate in the main to the activities which are initiated by the children themselves. As children widen their experience outside the home a variety of increasingly organised contexts, suggestions and challenges are likely to become more and more group and class-oriented.

The following guidelines, governing the selection of learning phases, are thought to be appropriate for a variety of situations in which 'assisted movement learning' takes place. They can be used by members of the family who engage in the early movement play of their children, by early childhood educators who cater for individuals and small groups, and by class teachers in the preparation and translation into more structured lessons. In all these settings it is important to keep the following points in mind.

- All phases are important in the movement development of children up to eight years.

- Not every movement session/lesson has to start with free exploration.

- There is not a special sequence – phases may be taken out of order and occur more than once.

- Phases may take up different lengths of time.

- Not all phases have to happen in one movement session/lesson.

- Phases may be combined.

The object now is to look at how phases may be used within several different learning/teaching situations. And at the same time to consider ways in which some of the theoretical notions introduced earlier tie up with the movement classification looked at in Chapter 1.

# A FLEXIBLE APPROACH

The general format for informal activity sessions at one end of the age range and directly structured lessons at the other have common threads although, as may be expected, the nature of the challenges set, the use of teaching devices, and child expectations are very different. However, there is nothing sacrosanct about every detail of content; some ideas are interchangeable although the treatment of them may differ. For example, the dance theme of fireworks as set out on pages 108–10 may be used in a different way with younger – or older – age groups. Similarly, the 'dance play' session, pitched at the level of three and four year-olds, which appears on pages 104–6 may be reshaped and extended in a variety of ways for children in infant and junior schools. It is the relationship of the various elements, along with the measure for potential development, which defines suitability in each case.

All spontaneous and structured activity sessions, along the lines of those which follow, contain what might be termed adult-led ingredients. These may be thought of as roles which parents, leaders and teachers take on, or as teaching styles, or simply as ways in which to enable maximum learning to take place. Adult-led ingredients are used here as structuring agents. They identify ways in which the most can be made of periods of children's activity whenever and wherever that activity may take place. It might be argued that common guidelines bring about inflexibility, but the opposite is true. The flexible use of phases of learning implies a knowledge both of child development and the educational and movement principles involved, whereby outcomes can be varied. Important elements in the examples given are:

- setting the scene;
- observing the outcome;
- giving feedback;
- engaging in dialogue.

## Making suggestions and setting challenges

Sometimes adults need to find ways to set children off; to stimulate, to lead, to interest, to involve them. Often this may be through the kinds of material provision talked about earlier. It may also come about through making suggestions as to what the children might do, or by talking about what they are in the process of doing. As cognitive, emotional and physical development advance the 'take it or leave it' type of suggestion, frequently used with young children who are working independently, is replaced by set and semi-set challenges which can be appropriately answered by all the children in a group or class.

In relation to early childhood education, the very idea of challenges, in the form of adult-led experiences, may seem rather prescriptive, daunting, even solemn. But in this context it is used to express the notion of potential achievement which children may set for themselves. A relevant, open-ended challenge encourages appropriate movement responses and, therefore, need hold no danger of children being unable to respond. In writing about open-ended versus closed structures, Bruce (1991, p. 89) draws attention to Jack, aged four years, who was asked to make a fish using a template and prescribed materials – milk bottle tops for scales and tissue paper for the tail. Personal decisions in Jack's fish activity were minimal and, in comparison, adult expectations of what the end product should look like were high. The movement equivalent of such an experience would be found in precisely fashioned skill sequences which do not enter into the early years of learning. 'The younger the child, the more the teacher, nursery nurse or auxiliary will need to concentrate on personalising and individualising the child's experiences (Wetton, 1988, Introduction).

At other times, rather than responding to expansive suggestions, interest is triggered by seeing other people, either children or adults, engaged in a particular form of movement. 'Children are affected by the context in which learning takes place, the people involved in it, and the values and beliefs which are embedded in it' (DES, 1990, paras 67–68).

## Observation

A central characteristic which comes to the fore, when considering children's learning in movement, is the adult's ability to observe quickly and accurately. Swift and informed observation means that assessment can be immediate, and feedback equally so. Without the help which arises from good observation techniques children can be 'strangleheld' in an activity for longer than is necessary or fulfilling. Writing of the importance of observation in physical education teaching, Underwood (1988, p. 5) writes:

> *On the basis of [these] observations, decisions will be made concerning the length of practice, the type of feedback to be given, whether to make comments to individuals, groups or the whole class.*

For example, a girl near to performing a backward somersault over a pole may just need to know that she should let her head go back with the rest of her upper body as she brings her legs up to the pole. To be told that she is nearly there but not quite making it because her head is restricting the circular passage of movement, and to receive instantaneous encouragement and help to put the words into practice, may mean that she meets with success 'sooner than later'. Such advice, support and encouragement, resulting from skilled observation, is in tune with a 'potential' level of development, suggested by Vygotsky (1978, p. 86) who writes:

> *the zone of proximinal development . . . is the distance between the actual development level as determined by independent problem solving and the level of potential development as determined through problem solving under adult guidance or in collaboration with more capable peers.*

Observation also provides material for long-term movement assessment and evaluation on which records and profiles are based. Hurst (Moyles ed. 1994, p. 173) presents an interesting view of the importance of observation in children's play. She writes of the challenge for early childhood educators to learn from observation and identifies purposes and procedures in the learning/teaching situation. There is no doubt about the general importance of this process but its practice within a field of experience like movement, which is transitory in nature, brings with it a particular set of problems which needs to be separately addressed. Apart from Chapter 6, where observation is the key issue, the examples of record-keeping based on movement observations given throughout this book necessarily refer to specific situations. However, there is also a general need for both early childhood and movement practitioners and theorists to examine the nature of this important aspect of recording, monitoring and assessing movement, at greater depth and in more detail. In this way movement will be more clearly seen to take its place alongside other areas of learning, sharing the common core to which Hurst refers but identifying its own 'peculiarities'.

## Looking and talking together

Whatever their age, wherever they may be, talking to the children about their movement is a major part of the learning situation. It provides the means whereby achievement and understanding can be assessed and it features prominently in the recording process too. The questions the adults and children ask, as well as help and guidance given to individuals and like-minded groups as they work, are of the utmost importance. They are times which are highly valued by children and adults alike. Consequently, looking and talking together is an ingredient included in all the examples which follow later. The time spent on talking together will vary, increasing in length as childrens' concentration spans expand.

Another significant factor influencing the manner in which children and adults look and talk together is in relation to 'whose movement it is'. With very young children their concentration, and their conversation, is predictably on 'me and my movement'. It may be some time before the movement of others is of lasting interest. However, it is useful to note the way in which children of the same age assist each other's learning in a manner not catered for in adult-child relationships (Blatchford et al. 1982, p. 3). Such evidence supports the view taken here that encouraging children to talk with each other about what is happening, and exchange views, is educationally sound.

We can see from the wide range of questions asked of the children in the sample activity sessions which follow that the notion of movement matching, referred to on page 89, operates equally in terms of language. Questions have to be of the right sort for the children to think about and answer in an appropriate manner. With the youngest children questions need to be tied, in some way, to the 'here and now' of their activity; to what is within their immediate grasp. They should be of a 'matter of fact' variety which can be shared with the adult present. Later on, most children of six years and older are able to surmise a little, to allow 'ifs' and 'buts' into their descriptions and conversations, and are able to deviate from the immediate situation. Meadows and Cashdan (1988, p. 59) point out that:

> whenever we ask a question we are making a 'demand' on that child ... The teacher who is aware of the range of possible levels of demand is in a good position to vary

*questions appropriately, striking the best balance between extending the child and consolidating their existing knowledge.*

One of the overriding values of language exchange within the movement session is the clarification and articulation of the skills and versatility the children are achieving; to describe both the process – what is taking place – and the end product, if there is one.

# Examples of sample activity sessions

What follows now is a set of movement activity sessions, any one of which might arise spontaneously with, or be specifically planned for, children up to eight years of age. In each case the situation is identified in the following terms:

- type of situation;
- resources;
- duration of activity;
- age of children;
- central movement ideas;
- learning phases;
- adult roles.

The most important resource of all, the adult who takes responsibility for the learning process, is shown through a variety of teaching strategies. These range enormously from involvement in the early activities of the youngest children right through to the class teacher in the junior school. The strategies include:

- the making of suggestions and setting of challenges;
- observations of general and specific kinds;
- looking and talking with the children;
- implementation of learning phases.

## The younger children

In the case of the two- and three-year-olds the major part of movement activity times will be started spontaneously by the children themselves or in response to the sort of provision made for them. At other times, joining in with parents or older brothers' and sisters' activities brings about enhanced understanding as well as a strong sense of camaraderie. Times such as these prove to be great favourites with the children as long as the main emphasis is on the 'doing', or perhaps what we might call 'me doing'. As we saw with Lucy's play session on pages 00–00, the adult's main concern at this time is to create the setting, and to 'accompany' the children in their learning, assisting this in as personal a way as possible.

   Because of the individual and somewhat unpredictable nature of childrens' movement 'happenings' at this early stage, the sample activity charts which follow will start for children around four years of age. Several individuals and groups of people will be involved in, and take responsibility for, movement activity sessions of the kind suggested here. They will all have some direct or indirect teaching component in what they do but the definition and extent of this will vary greatly according to the age of the children and the context in which the activity occurs. This could be in the home, or in a variety of group settings, ranging from family centres and play groups to nursery, infant and junior schools.

# SITUATION 1: SEIZING THE OPPORTUNITY

## For young children at home or in a variety of nursery settings

| | |
|---|---|
| **Resource** | Climbing frame with poles, ladders, planks, slides. |
| **Age** | About four years. |
| **Time** | 15 minutes or as long as interest lasts. |
| **Movement ideas** | The body: parts used to travel, actions used to travel. |
| **Learning phase** | Free exploration. |
| **Role of adult** | – To observe and comment generally and with individual children about what they are doing. |
| | – To draw attention to parts of the body and actions being used as they move. |
| | – To select two activities to be shown. |

Looking with the children, for example, at the following:

- one child travelling along plank on 'tummy', pulling along with hands;

- another child climbing the frame using hands and feet.

Talking with the children, who are asked to name and talk about:

- parts of the body being used;

- different ways they are used e.g. to pull along or climb.

| | |
|---|---|
| **Challenge** | Children asked to go back to where they were working, to move again in their 'special' way and to make it clear what parts of themselves they are using and what sorts of actions they are doing. |
| **Learning phase** | Consolidation. |
| **Role of adult** | – To observe and talk with the children about what they are doing. <br> – To direct comments to the way in which they are travelling and the parts of the body being used. |

## Situation 1 reviewed

Underlying a decision to work with young children in this way is the assumption that, at certain periods during the day, it is important for young children to have the opportunity to spend some time on the agility apparatus whether at home, at the play group, with the child-minder or at nursery school. It is a case of seizing the opportunity, of finding an appropriate period of time to become actively involved in the children's learning. The appropriateness, of course, relates both to the children and to the adult concerned who has to fit this in amongst the many other calls upon time, energy and attention.

We have seen from the activity chart above that the first task is to observe what the children are doing and how the information, gleaned from these observations, can best be used. This means making a mental assessment as the child travels around. Having decided on the movement ideas most in evidence, two examples can then be selected. Children of this age are not always able to reproduce, on request, what is wanted and it is a good idea to tell them to try and remember what they are doing because it may be shown to the other children later on. In this case, the two examples – and they are only examples – of travelling along the plank on the tummy and climbing the frame using hands and feet, were chosen.

The body with all its various connotations is an early and recurring frame of reference for young children. In looking at the two activities, the children are asked to name and talk about body parts involved and the actions performed. This gives them two things to keep in mind, which, because those two things are closely related, is just about right for children of this age. It is not chance that the two activities selected to be shown were very different from each other both in terms of the parts of the body involved and in the ways of moving. This allows ideas about 'different from' to be used to help the children describe the activities they were watching or doing.

In the second, consolidation, phase, the activity chart shows that the children are given a chance to concentrate once more on 'me and my movement'. They will be able to do this with greater understanding and clarity because of the shared looking, naming and describing activity which has just taken place. The ability of the adult to move around the group consolidating what has been, and is being, learned is an important part of the session. The time allocation of 'as long as interest is maintained' reflects the fact that at this age much of what goes on is an individual affair which may be longer, and more concentrated, for some individuals than for others.

# SITUATION 2: LISTEN AND MOVE

## For children at home or in a variety of nursery settings

| | |
|---|---|
| **Resource** | Uncluttered space inside or out. |
| **Age** | About four years. |
| **Time** | 10 minutes or so. |
| **Movement ideas** | The body: all parts working together with actions of going and stopping.<br>Space: on the spot and travelling. |
| **Challenge** | Listen to these words . . .<br>sssshake and sssshudder<br>sssshake and sssshudder<br>skim, skim and stop |

|  | Children asked to dance as words are spoken. |
|---|---|
| **Learning phase** | Adult-led experience. |
| **Challenge** | Children asked to practise separate parts as words are spoken:<br>(a) shaking and shuddering on spot;<br>(b) skimming all over the space;<br>(c) stopping very suddenly – in a new place. |
| **Role of adult** | Looking and talking together.<br>Two children show dances (one after the other) while adult talks about: |

- what they are doing;

- which bits are particularly well done;

- inviting children to join in the commentary, that is, giving a verbal accompaniment as the children dance.

| **Challenge** | Dancing the dance again. |
|---|---|
| **Learning phase** | Consolidation. |
| **Challenge** | Children asked to listen carefully to the words and then to join in with them, then asked to dance saying the words as they move. |
| **Learning phase** | Extension. |
| **Role of adult** | – To encourage 'the partnership' of words and dance.<br>– To be aware of children's own phrasing. |

## Situation 2 reviewed

Unlike Situation 1, where the adult lets the activity get under way before becoming actively involved, this period of 'dance play' entails getting one or two children, or a small group of individuals, together in a contained and containable space. Again two of the movement ideas relate to the body, while a third refers to the general space in which the activity is taking place.

This time the adult guides the movement responses. With the children in 'listening mode', he or she speaks the rhythmic phrases which provide both the stimulus and accompaniment. In order for the children to appreciate the rhythmic, flowing content of the words they need to be spoken with a feeling for the intrinsic phrasing and a sense of the whole. This does not necessarily come naturally and phrases often need to be well practised in order for them to be effective. Children will need help to get the shaking and shuddering into the whole of their bodies – from their heads to their toes. The main feature of the skimming activity is to travel across and through the space, although the way in which the word is spoken may suggest that this is done with light and quick movement. Stopping suddenly, always an excitement and delight in the very young, means cutting off their movement and finding themselves in a different place in the space. Perhaps they may be encouraged to think of it as a journey.

Once more, the second learning phase is one where the initial experience is consolidated, the difference, on this occasion, being that the end of the session is common to all the children participating.

# SITUATION 3: VERSATILITY AND SKILL IN GAMES

## For children in Year 2 of infant school

| | |
|---|---|
| **Resource** | Balls, bats, sticks, hoops, ropes, beanbags, rings, cones etc. |
| **Age** | Six to seven years. |
| **Time** | 25/30 minutes. |
| **Movement ideas** | The body: parts.<br>Space: directions. |
| **Challenge** | Children asked to collect the apparatus they were using in the previous lesson and practise making it move forwards or upwards. |
| **Learning phases** | Consolidation (apparatus being used).<br>Adult-led experience (use of directions). |
| **Role of adult** | To observe and comment generally, making sure children understand the task and helping them to identify their direction.<br>Looking with the children at, for example: |

- one child with rope skipping forwards;

- another child throwing and catching a rubber ring upwards.

Talking with the children about:

- the difference in direction;

- the same body parts being used;

- different actions.

| | |
|---|---|
| **Challenge** | Children asked to choose different apparatus and to find 'unusual ways' of making it move. |
| **Learning phase** | Adult-led experience. |
| **Role of Adult** | To observe and encourage individuals to experiment with 'out of the ordinary' parts of their bodies to make the apparatus move. |

Looking, for example, at:

- one child moving on front of body using the head to make ball move;

- a second child jumping with bean bag between the feet.

Talking about skill involved in both activities, for example:

- amount of control in keeping ball close to head;

- giving the body two jobs – to hold the bean bag in place and to jump well.

| | |
|---|---|
| **Challenge** | Children encouraged to make their activities more skilled and to be prepared to explain how they are doing this. |
| **Learning phase** | Consolidation. |

## Situation 3 reviewed

This session is directly structured and likely to exist as one of a series of lessons planned over a given length of time, perhaps four or five weeks. It takes into consideration the assumption that children of this age group will be able to remember what they were doing in the previous lesson – albeit in some cases with a bit of help. Secure in this knowledge the teacher can start with a phase of consolidation, in this case to ask the children to collect the apparatus they used the time before. The first learning phase, however, is a dual phase which, in addition to consolidation, features adult-led experiences. This time directions are used to help shape the children's activities; they are asked to make their apparatus move forwards or upwards. It is vital that sufficient time is allowed for their responses to this challenge, and indeed all challenges. In the time allotted to looking and talking together the children are asked to analyse two games, one going forward while skipping, and another showing the upward throwing and catching of a rubber ring. It is clear that these two distinctly different games activities are quite complex. In addition to highlighting the directional differences the teacher takes the opportunity to identify the skill factors needed in each. The lesson ends with the children re-working their games in the light of comments made.

# SITUATION 4: FIREWORK DANCES

## For children in Year 3 of junior school

| | |
|---|---|
| **Resource** | Hall or gymnasium. |
| **Age** | Eight years. |
| **Time** | 40 minutes. |
| **Movement ideas** | The body: actions.<br>Space: directions, pathways and patterns.<br>Dynamics: as related to individual fireworks.<br>Relationships: simple duo. |
| **Challenge** | Children asked to think of a firework and to show how it moves. |
| **Learning phase** | Adult-led experience. |
| **Role of adult** | To observe and talk with individuals, helping them to clarify their movement.<br>Looking, for example, at one rocket dance and one catherine wheel dance. |

Talking about what is different about:

- the pattern made straight/circular;

- the dynamics rapid start/spluttery end;

- the steady, continuous action/gradual slowing down.

Talking about what is the same:

- the three parts which make the whole.

| | |
|---|---|
| **Challenge** | Children asked to re-work their firework dance, paying attention to the three constituent parts of: |

(a) ignition;

(b) main activity;

(c) end.

| | |
|---|---|
| **Learning phase** | Consolidation. |
| **Role of adult** | To observe and talk to individuals, groups, the whole class, at appropriate intervals drawing attention to such things as: |

- when being ignited making the whole body come alive, ready to go into action;

- the best action for the firework e.g. running, jumping, turning;

- the most appropriate ending e.g. a slow fade out, a splutter, abrupt end.

Looking and talking together as half the class watch the others dancing to see:

- children whose dances show three clear phases;

- those who have clear patterns;

- those who have good rhythms.

Observers and dancers then change over.

| | |
|---|---|
| **Challenge** | Children asked to find a partner who dances a different firework. One child to dance firework, finishing near |

partner, the last spark setting second child alight who then dances his/her firework and finishes away from partner.

**Learning phase**     Extension.

**Teaching role**     Look with the children at firework dances in small groups.

## Situation 4 reviewed

Built into this lesson are the increased length of time children are able to concentrate, their ability to keep several things in mind at the same time, to reflect on their movement, and give and take with a partner. In asking the children to make up a firework dance the teacher assumes that they will be able to relate dynamic and spatial notions to appropriate actions of the body (see Chapter 1). One other important assumption is that the children's time concepts go beyond extremes of 'quick' and 'slow' to those of 'acceleration' and 'deceleration'. This involves a physical performance of the idea of seriation as discussed on page 14. In extending their observation abilities the idea of some things being the same and others different is introduced.

The partner dance is initially demanding but the composition is helped by the 'linking' factor, discussed fully in Chapter 6, in which one dancer ends beside the other and in doing so provides the stimulus for the second half of the dance to begin.

## STARTING, SUPPORTING, CHECKING AND RECORDING

Concentration on ways in which children's movement education can be supported, extended and enriched culminates here with a list of suggestions (Figure 52 on page 112) which may be given to children from three to eight years; to individuals, small groups or classes in either formal or informal situations. The list is a 'sample' collection of suggestions from one area of movement only, namely agility. It is tempting to suggest that it is for 'short term loan' only for the joy of this movement classification is that, once thoroughly digested, many, many more such lists may be collated for any type of movement activity. This particular collection starts with just one, and then two, movement ideas which develop in complexity in what is being asked of the children.

The object is, in the first instance, to provide some suggestions from which parents, early childhood educators and teachers can select what they think is most relevant. However, the list has other uses. It makes it possible to check for areas of movement not given recent attention – perhaps levels, or symmetry, or patterns. To check when these suspected omissions were last considered should be simply a task of looking back through the records. Records could show that certain areas have been over used and that well established and repeated patterns of movement need enlarging and developing along with the implementation of new ones. Most importantly perhaps, the suggested movement content could reinforce and 'flesh out' the dominant schemas being used elsewhere in the home, the play group, the nursery or the school. For example, a child who seems completely absorbed in 'over and under' behaviour may benefit from an immersion in movement situations which provide opportunities of a similar nature which will 'aid and abet' this particular aspect of learning (Athey, 1990).

The listed challenges do not have to be used as they appear here as predetermined ones and they can be even more open-ended. Alternatively, they can provide a basis from which to assess what is happening in young children's movement – what is taking place in terms of bodily activity, along with associated characteristics of space, dynamics and relationships. So, instead of suggesting that children try out certain tasks, the content of those tasks could be a focus of observation. Which children are finding lots of places to jump? Are there examples of children travelling backwards? Who is it who, for days now, has been showing delight in going up and down everything in sight? Adults have a lot to offer in following up these observations by means of supporting and extending them as well as 'spotting' those activities which are just emerging or are beginning to be shared.

Children enjoy responding to movement challenges wherever they happen to be. Sometimes they challenge themselves, sometimes they appreciate adults setting challenges and they frequently enjoy setting challenges for each other. The following activities may be those we can see happening freely all around us or, alternatively, they can form the basis of adult-led experiences.

| ACTIVITY | IMPLICATIONS |
|---|---|
| **Jumping** being practised in **one place**<br>**Body**: action | Need to do activity over and over again –<br>assimilatory activity |
| **Stretching** the body fully while moving<br>on the floor<br>**Body**: action and shape | Assimilatory behaviour |
| Moving on the apparatus using **only<br>hands and feet**<br>**Body**: parts emphasised and parts<br>restricted | Highlighting two parts and restricting<br>others |
| Travelling round the room with **one part**<br>of the body **leading the way**<br>**Body**: part leading | Need to 'line up' other parts of the body<br>as one part takes the lead |
| Movement where **both sides of the body**<br>are doing **the same thing**<br>**Body**: design | Sense of evenness and balance |
| **Balancing** on **different parts** of the body<br>**Body**: action and parts taking weight | Alignment of rest of the body according to<br>points of balance |
| **Climbing** in lots of **different places**<br>**Body**: action | Selecting places where activity can be<br>done |
| Moving on floor/apparatus on **hands** and<br>**feet** travelling in **one direction**<br>**Body**: part highlighted. **Space**: direction | Keeping two things in mind: (a) the body<br>and (b) the space |
| Going **under** and **over** the apparatus with<br>some things happening **slowly**, others **quickly**<br>**Space**: zone. **Dynamics**: time | Concentration on the 'how' and 'where' of<br>movement |
| Lots of activities on the floor **without<br>putting weight on feet**<br>**Body**: restriction of parts | Emphasis on the parts not being used |
| Finding ways of **passing each other**<br>**Relationship**: with partner | Having to adapt to partner – to negotiate<br>to share a common goal |
| Playing **follow my leader**<br>**Relationship**: duo – leading and<br>following | Adapting to leader's actions, pathway and<br>timing |

*Figure 52    A sample list of agility challenges*

# 6 A Matter of Expression

One of the major responsibilities of adults working with young children is effective and sensitive interaction. This sometimes arises spontaneously, and sometimes takes place over longer periods of time. However good and extensive provision for learning may be, however effectively each day is organised, however informed the 'curriculum', interpersonal relations are of prime importance. Being in tune with children and their thoughts and feelings is essential for maximum development in all areas of learning.

## Establishing the boundaries

As we turn now to look at the way in which children's movement is linked with emotional and expressive behaviour, it is important to stress that this chapter does not address personality theories. Neither is it concerned with body language theories, many of which are characterised by well-researched collections of signs and signals carrying prescribed meanings. In identifying the restrictive and separate nature of such categorisation Beattie (1987, p. 231) makes the point that:

> . . . the body popularisers do not deal with the continuity of behaviour. They do not give us advice about how to extract a particular act from the stream of behaviour. They offer instead a series of frozen frames with meanings attached . . .

In this chapter we are concerned with the stream of movement occurrences as we look at the part movement plays in the expression of personality. Put in another way, we are going to look at how personality can be assessed in movement terms. The relationship of movement to emotional and expressive behaviour is central to what follows. North (1972, p. 12) writes:

> If we accept that the way people sit, walk and make gestures has any relevance to how they are thinking and feeling, then it is only a short step towards the idea that a more subtle and deep analysis of the composition of the movement can lead towards a greater understanding of the personality.

It is also important to stress that this book does not intend to look at the complexity of the observation and interpretation of movement phrases and clusters or of the in-depth study of human movement itself. Those wishing to learn more should refer to the works of Laban and the many educationalists, therapists and movement specialists who have contributed to this immense field of study. They are too numerous to mention here but their publications feature throughout the text and are included in the bibliography.

However, as North (1972, p. 12) suggests, 'It is common knowledge that we are all observers of movement, and that we all draw conclusions from our observations of other people.' She indicates that there is much that can be done by the non-specialist in this field. After all, those who are concerned with the care and education of young children are already tried and tested in the art not only of looking but of seeing. As Lally (1991, p. 87) points out, teachers and nursery nurses are trained both to observe and to learn from observation and 'are constantly intent on improving their practice'. Neither is it necessarily the case, that to be a good observer one has to be a gifted mover. This is particularly true in the area of movement expression and in support of such a claim, Lawrence (1947, p. xv) writes:

> To be a good observer of other persons' effort-expressions, one need not oneself have great bodily expressiveness. Good movers may be poor observers, and may even be unable to notice evident rhythm in larger movements.

## ALL MOVEMENT IS EXPRESSIVE

All movement, however small, is a means of expressing and communicating whereby children, through their self-selective patterns, show themselves as unique individuals. The expressive nature of movement applies not only to descriptive gestures but also to functional and utilitarian tasks. 'All movement is expressive, even the most functional' is a view expressed by Laban (1947) and endorsed by other movement specialists and educationalists since that time. It is especially important in considering the expressive behaviour of young children.

Although children employ highly differentiated combinations of movement ingredients there are, of course, some, but not all, which are common to specific situations. Children adopt similar patterns of waving; they nod and shake their head using common directions; they embrace and kiss in roughly the same way. But even within those common patterns there are clearly observable cultural and social norms, as well as individual differences, all of which play their part in shaping what takes place.

## Moods and movement

Movement does not, by any means, tell everything we may wish to know about the things children are attempting to express or communicate. However, as one type of indicator, it is an invaluable contributor. For example, movement acts as a support system of nonverbal communicative signals which can be added to our use of linguistic and prelinguistic indicators (Whitehead, 1990, p. 18).

As well as individual shapes and shadings, there are certain general dynamic forms and patterns common to most children in the expression of moods such as anger, excitement, anxiety and distress and it may be helpful to look at these first. At some time or other we have all seen our children engage in moments of an expressive nature along the lines of the following:

- jumping for joy;
- shaking with excitement;
- inching forward cautiously;
- holding back with reticence;
- hitting out in anger;
- slumping in dejection;
- rising to the occasion;
- digging in their heels;
- throwing themselves whole-heartedly – or whole-bodily – into the game.

Looking at these examples we can see that through actions (jumping and shaking) and body parts (heels and toes) the body clearly remains a central feature of expressive activity. Directions such as forward, backward, upward and downward are there too along with their spatial counterparts of rising and sinking, advancing and retreating. However, the qualitative element, indicating *how* the activities are coloured or dynamically charged, is more implicitly conveyed. Reticence and caution imply restraint through the presence of bound flow. Hitting out suggests strength as does the digging in of heels. The excitement of jumping for joy could be said to be tinged with a sense of lightness, even light-heartedness. Relationships, in these examples, are also a matter of implication. There could be someone at the receiving end of hitting out. The reticent withholding may be in relation to the stranger who has just appeared on the scene.

## Making a note of it

There are more descriptions in everyday use which carry movement connotations than we perhaps imagine. The newspapers, and character portraits in literature, are full of examples. Nearer home are numerous phrases with which we describe the children in our care. We can base descriptions on movement expression, and this gives insight and understanding. Making notes of consistent, as well as irregular and unusual, movement-stressed occurrences is an important way of recording expressive movement behaviour and, over a longer period of time, its development. In the first instance, this can be done by recording very simple and uncomplicated expressions of mood and feeling states such as resentment, tenderness, or excitement. Using a simple chart similar to figure 53, information about the number and nature of significant expressive situations in respect of individual children can be swiftly assembled. Gathering of data of this kind will eventually result in building an informative picture of individual children and the interpretative outcomes can be used 'to support and extend learning' (Bartholomew and Bruce, 1993, p.87). Other, more detailed ways of recording expressive movement appear later in the chapter.

## Personal style

Although commonly expressed feelings clearly have movement connotations, it is not true to say that anger always produces tightening of the muscles and hard-hitting action while happiness is expressed by large, exuberant and expansive movement. Among any set of children there will be those whose expression of happiness is quiet and still, and those whose anger may be wild and loose-limbed or cool and contained. To suggest that specific movement equals feeling would be a mistake. It would dismiss the whole idea of personal style and its relationship to social and cultural norms. North (1972, p. 35) summarises in the following way:

> It is impossible to say either that a particular movement equals a special quality or that a special quality equals one movement pattern . . .

| JASON | MOODS AND MOVEMENT CHART | |
|---|---|---|
| **DATE** | MOOD/EXPRESSIVE ACTIVITY<br>What does his/her movement say? | COMMENTS |
| 11/5 | Excitement – high level of agitation – seen on and off throughout the day. Rushing boisterously around. Changing from one action to another – running, jumping, spinning, jigging up and down. Laughing loudly. | It is his fourth birthday and he is having a party when he gets home! |
| 13/5 | Temper tantrum – on arrival at the nursery. Tight body, clenched fists, stamping feet. Clung hard to mother and dragged right back from her as she brought him through the door. Didn't communicate with anyone at first but gradually eased. | Most unusual occurrence – difficult to know why this happened. He did have one setback yesterday when he couldn't use the slide when he wanted. Will have a word with father when he collects him. *1 |
| | | |
| | | |

*1 Jason's father explained that Jason wanted to accompany his parents who were going to visit his grandparents for the day. Jason often stayed overnight when he went to visit and he was worried in case his mother and father didn't get back in time to collect him.

*Figure 53    A sample 'moods and movement' chart*

In the momentary absence of swans and geese on the river, two-and-a-half-year-old Perry spent a busy time feeding the pigeons which gathered regularly on the bridge. His movement was generally outgoing and free as he pursued them with his bread. Then suddenly he saw a swan and for one moment sheer excitement made him stop absolutely still in his tracks. His body narrowed and all parts came immediately to his centre. His hands covered his mouth, his eyes almost closed, and even his toes appear to turn up as, seeming to hug the excitement to himself, he looked at the swan – the pigeons for the moment forgotten. His excitement and delight, seen in figure 54 being shared by his family, were soon replaced by his previous boisterous, action-packed behaviour as he returned again to his friendly pursuit of the pigeons. Although Perry's expression is clear and meaningful, in a different context it could have signified something different.

*Figure 54    Excitement shown by Perry, aged two*

With Jake, aged five, excitement is expressed in a quite different way as he achieves the moment of greatest height on the see-saw. His total body attitude is one of expansion, his legs are wide astride, his chest is wide open and his mouth too! The mood is one of large, freely flowing joy. The only sign of restraint and binding of flow is an appropriate one as Jake controls his position on the see-saw with his hands.

*Figure 55    Excitement shown by Jake, aged five*

Examining the link between movement and feeling Borten (1963) writes, in poetic vein, about the variety of expression which can be associated with moving backward:

*Backward-going movement can shrink in fear,*
*recoil in disgust, or spring back in surprise.*
*It can be as stingy as a miser's closing fist*
*or as cold and unsociable as an oyster*
*drawing into its shell. When I move backwards,*
*I am a cat cringing in terror . . .*
*or a flower closing its petals against the frosty night air.*

And moving forwards:

> *Forward-going movement can be open*
> *and giving ... but it can push and take*
> *too, like a child grabbing toys from*
> *his playmate. It can be sassy as*
> *a stuck-out tongue, or as impulsive*
> *as a leap in the dark. It can be as*
> *bold as a punch in the nose, or*
> *as menacing as a tidal wave.*

Most children, but not all, express themselves freely and fully. They leave little doubt about how they feel in the minds of those 'in charge' – or those who just happen to pass through their sphere of expressive activity. At certain times, and with some children, the movement expression is less obvious and it is necessary to look more closely in order to decipher the messages being unconsciously, or intentionally, conveyed. But, whether full-blown or understated, the movement phrases of young children, and the colourful analytical phrases which describe them, are clearly articulated.

# THE CLASSIFICATION OF MOVEMENT RE-VISITED

In order to delve a little deeper into the significance of the relationship between children's movement and their emotional and expressive development we need to have the categories of movement in the forefront of our minds. It would be helpful, therefore, to look back and refresh memories of the original classification on pages 1–24 which gives detailed information about:

- *what* moves – the body;

- *how* it moves – the expressive quality involved;

- *where* it moves – within and outside its own special space;

- *with whom* or *with what* it relates – the people and objects which fill the day.

## Making an 'effort': how children move

Of special importance here is the second section of the classification which refers to how children move. This category of dynamically-emphasised movement is widely known as 'effort' (Laban 1947). It is a classification of movement elements which, according to Redfern (1973, p. 37), 'is of particular importance in the realm of dance and movement expression'. Attention was drawn in Chapter 1 to the ways in which movement is dynamically charged and structured, and suggestions were made as to how movement needs to be appropriately coloured in order to be effective and expressive. Those explanations are particularly important in the consideration of expressive movement functioning, and another look at pages 11–14 will prove helpful at this point. However, because this part of the classification is especially relevant to the expressive and emotional make-up of young children it is given additional consideration within this chapter.

## The four motion factors: a general overview

To gain even more insight into this area of movement we should look now more closely at the motion factors – weight, qualitative space, time and flow.

### Weight
The weight factor of movement gives rise to a fine, sensitive manner of moving at one end of the continuum through to one of strength and firmness at the other.

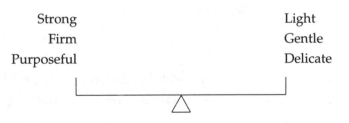

Strong           Light
Firm           Gentle
Purposeful           Delicate

*Figure 56    The weight factor*

Because the weight factor is associated with actual tension in the muscles, it is called the physical component. Laban links it with intention. In general terms one person can be heard to say of another 'she takes a firm stand' or 'he only touched lightly on that subject'. Each of these comments says something about people acting in certain situations just as this observation says something about three-year-old Alison when she was called in from the garden where she was playing. She folded her arms, plonked her feet apart and said 'no' firmly and loudly, indicating that she had every intention of staying just where she was.

## Qualitative space

The space factor of qualitatively stressed movement (not to be confused with the medium of space indicating where movement takes place) gives rise to elements of flexibility through to directness.

This motion factor is linked with attention. It is associated with the capacity to hone in or to pinpoint. At the other end of the continuum there is a flexible all-roundness in the expression indicating consideration of all sides of a situation. Sophie, aged two, illustrates this well for us. When she is painting, a special interest of hers, she is quite unaware of all the other things going on around her. She gives her painting her undivided attention until she wants to do something else.

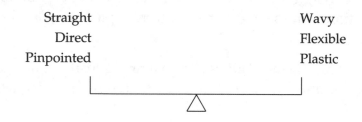

Straight  Wavy
Direct  Flexible
Pinpointed  Plastic

*Figure 57    The qualitative space factor*

## Time

Time, the third motion factor, is associated with decisiveness and the range of expressive activity here is reflected between the elements of suddenness and sustainment.

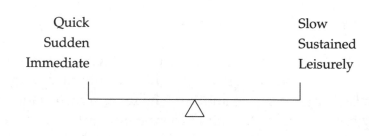

Quick  Slow
Sudden  Sustained
Immediate  Leisurely

*Figure 58    The time factor*

Sudden, abrupt, quick movement is typical of those people who act and re-act with immediacy. Characteristics of leisure and unhurried pace are typical of those who take a long time to come to a decision or judgement of any kind. Tariq, aged five and at infant school, displays a strong sense of suddenness. When his teacher asks a question Tariq is always ready to leap in with the answer. He does not pause to think before deciding to respond and he sometimes forgets what he wants to say – that is if he always has something to say in the first place!

## Flow

Flow, the last of the four motion factors, is the most complex one. This is because it has a dual role. It is linked on the one hand with *precision* of action and, on the other, with *communication*.

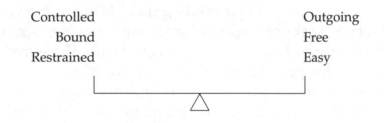

Controlled                Outgoing
Bound                Free
Restrained                Easy

*Figure 59    The flow factor*

It is concerned, therefore, with the care and control used in carrying out everyday acts. It is also about the making, breaking and withholding of relationships. Free flow is characterised by the outgoing nature of movement, with ease and lack of restriction, and bound flow by a certain stickiness and caution. There is no sign of stickiness or caution in Gavin's behaviour. He is a good communicator. He loves being with people and people enjoy being with him. Whenever anyone new comes into the nursery he is among the first to get acquainted.

At this point it is worth re-iterating the need to recognise the value-free nature of movement elements in their own right. Both aspects, and all the degrees between the two, are positive. Only if they are used inappropriately, or in an exaggerated manner, can they be said to be negative. All children have natural preferences and it is these sets of preferences which give them their individuality. As North (1972, p. 27) comments:

*If we look at the variety and range of patterns and rhythms of the movement of many people, we find that each configuration is personal, individual, different.*

# ASSESSING EXPRESSIVE BEHAVIOUR

Central to the notion of motion factors is the idea that movement takes place on a continuum rather than being seen as two polarities such as 'sudden' and 'sustained'. The sense of being moderately sustained, extremely sudden or hardly registering a time sense at all – that is operating in a somewhat neutral area – are all possibilities of differentiation. Important too is the implication that movement can range between and within personal limits.

Trained movement observers would be able to establish fine degrees of differentiation as to where on each of the 'scales' individuals are functioning. Most importantly, they would then relate these to the other three factors, namely, the body, the space and relationships. Such detailed observations, along with their interpretations, would be of particular significance to psychologists and therapists working with clients needing specialist help. However, there are relevant, and relatively simple means of assessing the expressive status quo of young children in terms of movement which can be used effectively and which will give support to the general compilation of records.

The following movement profiles of Shobana (three years) and Timothy (five years) use observations related specifically and exclusively to the four motion factors of weight, time, qualitative space and flow. The four 'markers' used in making the placements are:

⌒    the range of movement expression;

☐    the extent to which a quality is experienced;

○    the extent to which the complementary quality is experienced;

△    the fulcrum signifying a somewhat neutral area. The nearer movement is to the fulcrum the less pronounced it is.

## Shobana's movement profile

What do these observations tell us about Shobana's movement?

(a) Shobana moves very gently. She is extremely delicate in what she does (near the end of the continuum). However, in contrast, she has very little at her disposal in terms of strong and forceful qualities (her placement in terms of strength is only just the other side of the fulcrum).

(b) In terms of spatial quality, Shobana shows that she is able to perform with a

Strong                         Light
Firm                           Gentle
Purposeful                     Delicate

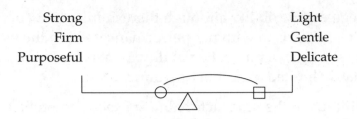

(a)   WEIGHT

Straight                       Wavy
Direct                         Flexible
Pinpointed                     Plastic

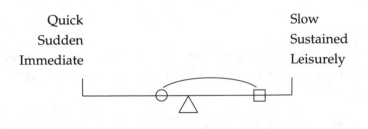

(b)   QUALITATIVE SPACE

Quick                          Slow
Sudden                         Sustained
Immediate                      Leisurely

(c)   TIME

Controlled                     Outgoing
Bound                          Free
Restrained                     Easy

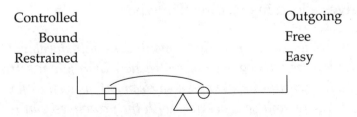

(d)   FLOW

*Figure 60    Shobana, aged three years*

considerable degree of flexibility although there is still plenty of room for development. In comparison with her performance within the weight factor she has a slightly less extensive range. Her ability to carry out direct and straight movements is fairly limited (near the fulcrum).

(c) Shobana's attitude to the time factor almost exactly resembles her weight factor. She is predominantly a slow, sustained mover with little evidence at this stage of being able to produce much in the way of quick, abrupt movement.

(d) In terms of flow the emphasis of Shobana's movement is restrained and tightly controlled. Her ability to be free and more abandoned, as shown by her nearness to the fulcrum, is minimal.

### Linking records

Having made a current record of Shobana's qualitative movement range we can now see if these observations relate to other recordings of activities in which she participates. Observations and records which concur with each other give additional substance to the information base relating to individual children. Likewise, those which vary to any significant extent will provide scope for discussion, further investigation and consideration of short- and long-term plans for development. Bartholomew and Bruce (1993, p. 21) suggest that:

> We need a better cross-linking and getting-together of records about individual children along with the notes we keep on organisation, planning and provision.

If movement observation and recording are new ventures for early childhood educators it may be worthwhile to start as a team. Observing a child's movement and discussing it is one way of achieving a degree of objectivity and a sound way of establishing common principles. Drummond (1993, p. 150) gives a lead in this direction when she writes:

> Trust and respect for each other's judgements will only develop when there are opportunities for open dialogue between teachers in different settings, opportunities for genuine debate and disagreement, as well as for agreement and accord. The dialogue will be concerned with the principles that underlie effective assessment as well as with the day to day practice.

In an attempt to assess if the movement observations of Shobana are relevant to other narrative information, descriptions of her participation in domestic play and outside activities are given next and the movement correlations of these considered.

## Shobana: domestic play

Shobana spent some time looking round trying to choose what to do. She eventually decided to wash and dress her family of dolls. She handled each one of them with care, not being rough when she washed them and combing their hair carefully and gently.

The movement clues to take account of in this description are as follows.

| | |
|---|---|
| **Weight:** | The *intention* stress was in the gentle, sensitive handling of the dolls with no sign of roughness. |
| **Qualitative space:** | A flexible *attention* was seen in her looking around while considering what to do. Then she directed *attention* to the task in hand and kept her concentration fixed. |
| **Time:** | A leisurely *decision* – she took her time. |
| **Flow:** | Care and precision characterised the *control* which was exercised in combing the doll's hair. |

## Shobana: outside activity

Shobana expressed a wish to skip and was guided to where the ropes were kept. After a few minutes trying to make the rope go over her head she gave up – she 'did not really want to do it' she said. After wandering around the play area she eventually decided to use the slide. Ian, impatient with her slow ascent up the ladder, tried to push in front. Shobana just allowed herself to be pushed aside and, as was often the case with Shobana at this stage, she didn't attempt to stand up for herself. She seemed quite upset and it was some time before she cautiously approached a group of children who were gardening. Although there was no apparent problem she didn't really communicate with them and played on the outskirts of the group.

In terms of Shobana's outdoor activity we can see the following evidence of movement expression.

| | |
|---|---|
| **Weight:** | There were two instances where she lacked a sufficiently strong *intention*. The first was in really getting to grips with her skipping. She made only a light-hearted attempt. The second was in not taking a strong stand when Ian pushed in front of her. |

**Qualitative space:**     Again Shobana looked at what she would do next
before she gave the slide – and later the children – her
attention.

**Time:**     There was nothing quick about her *decision* to use the
climbing frame and although she didn't stay around
neither did she rush away from the scene of
confrontation. She was slow to recover from Ian's
intervention and took her time before going to join the
children gardening.

**Flow:**     Shobana did not *communicate* freely with the children she
joined, preferring to 'keep herself to herself'.

## Timothy's movement profile

We look now at a movement profile of Timothy and, as we did with Shobana,
watch out for supporting, or conflicting, evidence in descriptive passages of him
in a dance session and outside in the playground.

What do these observations tell us about Timothy's movement?

(a) Timothy's movement patterns show strength – he moves with purpose.
Although slightly less developed than his firmness he shows a good degree
of more delicate, sensitive movement. In fact within the weight factor he
shows a good range.

(b) Spatially Timothy is more flexible than direct. The reasonably well-
developed plasticity of movement is not complemented to the same degree
by the linear, straight aspect.

(c) Timothy's time range is wide. Although he shows a slight preference for
sudden, abrupt movement he is also able to move with a slow, more
leisurely quality.

(d) In terms of flow Timothy has a good capacity for freely flowing,
unrestrained, outgoing movement. He can also produce a controlled
and precise quality although this is a slightly less developed area of
expression.

### Timothy: the dance lesson

The teacher, who was introducing the idea of 'a dance of the autumn leaves',
suggested that the children should show leaves being blown along the ground

Strong                                 Light
Firm                                   Gentle
Purposeful                             Delicate

(a)   WEIGHT

Straight                               Wavy
Direct                                 Flexible
Pinpointed                             Plastic

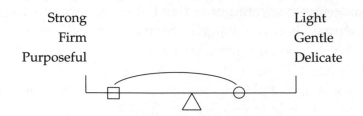

(b)   QUALITATIVE SPACE

Quick                                  Slow
Sudden                                 Sustained
Immediate                              Leisurely

(c)   TIME

Controlled                             Outgoing
Bound                                  Free
Restrained                             Easy

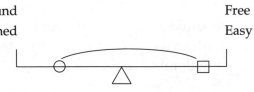

(d)   FLOW

*Figure 61    Timothy, aged five years*

and into the air. Timothy went immediately into action, hurling himself about the room with great abandon which bordered on a lack of control. However, he showed remarkably good judgement in avoiding collisions, weaving himself in and out of the other children with great skill. When asked to stop he was among the first to do so. When exploring being blown slowly and gently along the ground Timothy was able to manage this too.

The movement correlations to take account of in this description are:

**Weight:**   Implicit in the description of Timothy 'hurling' himself is the suggestion of strong *intention*. It almost gives the impression of being rough which can be a mis-use or exaggeration of strength. The description also tells us that Timothy is able to produce gentler movement.

**Qualitative space:**   The *attention* given to the flexibility of his body as he manoeuvred around the space and the other children reflected the thinking element connected with the space factor.

**Time:**   There is no doubt about Timothy's *decision* to move. It was abrupt and immediate. His response to the challenge to stop showed an equally quick response to the time factor. His ability to produce a slow, more leisurely quality shows that his range within the time factor is also quite well developed.

**Flow:**   The abandon with which Timothy set off signifies a personal delight in freely flowing, unrestrained movement where it could be said 'caution was thrown to the winds'. Like his strength, Timothy almost overdoes his free flow. One senses that with just a little more he would become 'out of control'. Yet we are assured that the *control* is there when necessary. The way in which he was able to 'put on the brakes' in order to avoid bumping into the other children showed that when he wanted he could employ considerable restraint.

## Timothy: in the playground

Timothy seemed in constant demand on this occasion, with other children eager for him to play with them. He responded easily and quickly to them and, most of the time, seemed to join in sensitively with what they were doing. Occasionally he seemed to have to make his mark and was very tough with them. He got really angry. His interest did not last long and soon he was off somewhere else.

The movement correlations to take account of here are:

**Weight:** Leaving his mark indicates a certain power or strength in relating to the other children – his *intention* was to lead. There is a tendency here, shown also in the dance session, for his strength to be almost over the top. Such occasions seem to be sporadic, however, and he also shows sensitivity and gentleness.

**Qualitative space:** This was not particularly emphasised in this situation.

**Time:** Timothy's attitude to time was shown in swift and immediate action and reaction in *deciding* when to join and when to leave a group.

**Flow:** His outgoing personality is a bonus in *communicating* with others. There is no feeling of holding back.

## Some other accounts of record-keeping

Movement observations of the kind used for Shobana and Timothy do not need to be made too often – probably about every two or three months is about right. It may be a good idea to have an observation sheet prepared, however, in case something remarkable occurs in between.

Accounts from other areas of record-keeping will not always be so specifically 'movement conscious' as those created on the previous pages. These were designed especially to show a maximum amount of possible connections. Some records will not suggest any correlations at all. Others may pick out one very important, or perhaps recurring, characteristic such as this one taken from Bartholomew and Bruce (1993, p. 62).

> *Connor's lack of confidence makes him a bit tentative to approaching new activities – he needs adult encouragement to be drawn into different/novel situations – he loves things that are familiar e.g. he knows all about dinosaurs and feels very secure when holding forth about them. His approach to learning is a bit like his approach to strange food – he is highly suspicious and wary.*

The whole of this most enlightening record draws attention to Connor's bound flow. The operative words are 'lack of confidence', 'tentative', 'suspicious' and 'wary'. However, free flow is obviously available to Connor, shown when dealing with familiar things. In this situation, as the record tells us, 'he is very secure'.

A similar record is provided by Lally (1991, p. 34) who writes of John, aged three years and ten months:

> John was a gentle, articulate child. He was [also] very capable of attending to his own physical needs but he was less confident about using the nursery environment. He sometimes seemed nervous of some of the other children, particularly the more boisterous ones, and was unable to stand his ground if another child challenged him for a piece of equipment – in these situations he would let the other child have the toy and move quickly away from the area.

As in Connor's case, this record tells of the presence of bound flow indicated in terms of being 'less confident' and 'nervous'. There is no indication in this observation, however, that free flow was also one of his characteristics. But there are clues that, in terms of weight, he is considered to be a gentle boy (a positive statement) but, conversely, that he was unable to take a 'firm stand' in the face of confrontation. His time sense is working well – he was quick to get away from the source of conflict!

## THE BROADER PICTURE: A COMPREHENSIVE MOVEMENT PROFILE

In this recent set of examples concentration is on the dynamically-emphasised, 'effort' category of movement, which plays a major role in expressive action. However, as confidence and skill in movement observation and recording grow, it is possible to look at small groups of clues, rather than single components. It is the relationship of all four motion factors – weight, qualitative space, time and flow – which gives the most comprehensive picture. However, observations increase in meaning even more when the 'how' of movement is related to the other three categories of movement classification, namely, the body, the medium of space, and relationships.

The following movement profile of Peter, aged five, illustrates the way in which attention to all four categories of movement can be given. An analysis is provided in figure 62 so that the movement implications can be recognised with ease. Clearly, it is a profile which has been intentionally constructed to include as many movement implications as possible. Its place here is mainly for reference purposes.

## Peter's movement profile

Peter is fairly tall for his age, has a narrow chest, and frequently *stands on one leg with the other foot turned in*. He often *lacks the drive* to get the most out of a piece of work. He *works slowly and carefully* at his self-chosen activities, often with *a feeling of leisure*. In the use of scrap materials he has made several models and in each case he has been able to *examine the possibilities of the various materials* on hand in his attempts to make his models 'just right'. Having finally chosen what he needs he disregards the other things and *focuses on the task in hand*, preferring at this stage *to work on the floor* and *well away from any of the other children*. At the beginning of term, Peter was very interested in the hamster but was rather *rough and heavy-handed*, holding it very *tightly*. Sometimes Peter gets upset and after such occasions he needs time and *space* to get over this by himself, *usually sitting on the floor* or *behind the door*. *If anyone comes near him* at these times he either *hits out at them* or *curls up into a ball, covering his face with his hands* and *holding his breath*. Lately, he has been much *gentler with the animals* and spends a lot of time *stroking their fur*. This seems *to relax him a little*. He shows *a similar gentleness* when he takes on the role of father. It is interesting to note that he can also *play tough roles* as he does when he is the man *clamping the cars*. In his outdoor activities Peter excels. He can *run and jump well* for his age and is able to *control both the force and direction of his kick*. Above all, he is exceptionally *expert at dodging, he can twist and turn while on the run and changes direction easily*. Peter is making good progress but he still appears *reticent and lacking in confidence* at times. He is *not easy to talk to* and has *few close friends* although many of the children go out to him freely. He *keeps very much to himself* and prefers to work *in one place in the room*. However, through Peter's natural reserve, there are *signs of letting go* and he *appears more expansive* recently.

# THE PURPOSE OF DETAILED MOVEMENT OBSERVATION

Detailed movement observation tells us something important about the development of children's emotional and expressive behaviour. Effective observation relies on the teacher's ability to 'observe each child as an individual and part of the group, analyse and evaluate each observation, identify the significant aspects of each observation and use the information gained to inform her approach to each child' (Lally, 1991, p. 92).

Observation specifically related to movement helps adults, in whatever

| DESCRIPTION | MOVEMENT IMPLICATIONS | |
|---|---|---|
| stands on one leg with other foot turned in | BODY: | design – asymmetry |
| lacks the drive | EFFORT: | weight – firm *intention* missing |
| works slowly ... | EFFORT: | time – work pattern is slow and leisurely |
| and carefully | | flow – which is precise and controlled |
| a feeling of leisure | EFFORT: | time – a hint of being laid back |
| examine the possibilities of the various materials | EFFORT: | qualitative space – a flexible, wide-ranging *attention* |
| focuses on the task in hand | EFFORT: | qualitative space – directs *attention* specifically to task |
| to work on the floor | SPACE: | level – low |
| well away from any of the other children | SPACE: | keeps himself to himself |
| rough and heavy-handed ... tightly | EFFORT: | weight – firm quality (mis-use) |
| needs space to get over it | SPACE: | needs personal space, to be un-invaded |
| usually sitting on the floor | SPACE: | level – low |
| behind the door | SPACE: | zone – door in front of him, separating him from others or as protection |
| if anyone comes near him | SPACE: | personal space under threat |
| | RELATIONSHIPS: | disallowed |
| hits out at them | EFFORT: | weight – strong *intention* |
| | BODY: | action – hits |
| | RELATIONSHIP: | at other children |
| curls up into a ball ... | BODY: | shape – all parts coming to the centre |
| covering his face with his hands | BODY: | articulation – hands used to prevent contact |
| holding his breath | EFFORT: | flow – bound (exaggerated use of restraint) |
| gentler with the animals | EFFORT: | weight – light and delicate handling |
| | RELATIONSHIP: | with animals |
| stroking their fur | BODY: | action – stroking |
| | EFFORT: | weight – gentle (implied) |
| to relax him a little | EFFORT: | weight – release of strong tension |
| a similar gentleness | EFFORT: | weight – fine, light touch |
| play tough roles ... clamping the cars | EFFORT: | weight – strong *intention* |
| run and jump well | BODY: | action – run and jump |
| control both the force | EFFORT: | weight – strong |
| | | flow – bound/free precision |
| ... and direction of his kick | SPACE: | direction – to make it go where needed |
| expert at dodging ... can twist and turn, while on the run | BODY: | action can combine actions |
| changes direction easily | EFFORT: | qualitative space – channelled |
| | | flow – fluent and free |
| reticent and lacking in confidence ... not easy to talk to | EFFORT: | flow – bound, restrained, withdrawn |
| few close friends ... keeps very much to himself | EFFORT: | flow – bound, cautious |
| | SPACE: | prefers personal space – not willing to let 'others in' |
| in one place in the room | SPACE: | prefers personal place |
| signs of letting go ... | EFFORT: | flow – increase of free flow – out-going |
| appears more expansive | BODY: | design – wider, more open |

*Figure 62    An analysis of the movement implications of Peter's profile*

capacity they function, to know the children better. It gives information about:

- children's personal movement style;

- the range of dynamic expression;

- preferred patterns of moving;

- exaggerated areas of movement expression;

- mis-used or inappropriate movement expression.

These are observations on which to build both short- and long-term learning processes. Like all good learning, development starts from where the children are, using their arrival platforms for departures of all kinds. For the younger children, provision plays a large part. Timothy, who so enjoyed the freely flowing, fast moving 'autumn leaves' dance experience on page 130 may well learn to employ different qualities and actions when moving with a balloon or to a piece of light, slow, lyrical music. Peter's tendency to 'hit out' (page 133) may be used legitimately in a dance where the hands and feet first punch and disturb the air and are then used to smooth it down again. Much has been said already about suitable stimuli and appropriate provision and the theme will be taken up again in the last chapter which explores the notion of expression within the context of dance.

## The 'movement repertoires' of parents, carers and teachers

Most occupations need a fairly extensive working movement vocabulary in order to carry out respective jobs with relevance and effectiveness. Teachers and carers in particular need a wide span of movement expression. Coping with and responding to sometimes as many as twenty or thirty different 'personality styles' requires expertise. The adult may need to be sensitive to one, take a firm stand with another, be aware of all the different things going on around while giving undivided attention to an individual child, know when to hold back, give out, let things take their time or react immediately. The demands are many.

Many other occupations also need a varied response. Take, for example, the 'lollipop' men and women who see a similar collection of children safely across the road. They too have to be appropriate in the ways in which they act and react. So what is the difference? Essentially it lies in the context which, for the road safety warden, is more limited in purpose and outcome and, therefore, more predictable. Different children have to be responded to, so too does the traffic flow and road conditions but the situation is contained in space (the crossing and immediate environment) and limited in time (arrivals and departures of the children). The teaching of older children, and certain subject specialisms, similarly call on less in terms of a wide range of movement expression. Certainly, the younger the children, and the freer the situation in which they function, the greater the variety of interaction between them and their carers and educators.

## Children observe adults too

'Infants and children out of school are [also] experts at reading the kinesic [non-verbal] messages given out, quite involuntarily, by their parents, minders and teachers' (Whitehead, 1990, p. 18). Figure 63 below is how David, aged four, describes his mother. He writes about actions and moods and conveys a convincing picture.

Figure 64 on page 137 is what Amy, aged seven, has to say about her teacher. Notice the number of movement – and implied movement – references here and the way in which Amy contrasts moods.

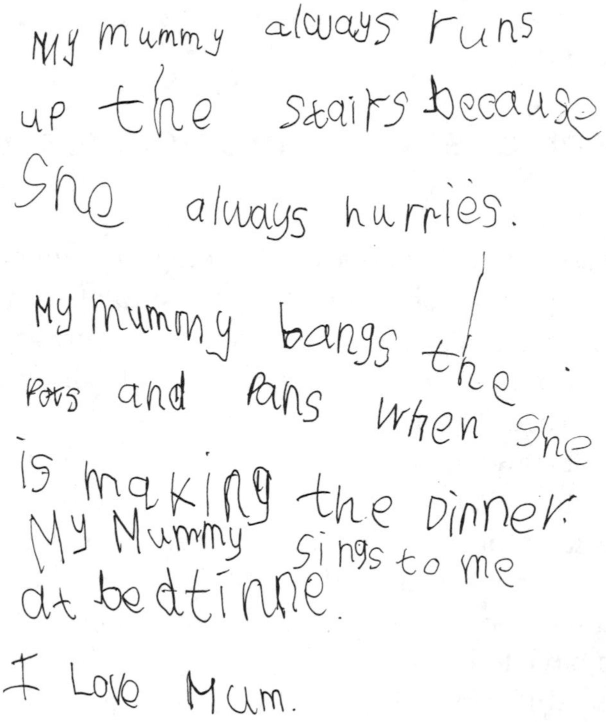

My mummy always runs
up the stairs because
she always hurries.

My mummy bangs the
pors and pans when she
is making the Dinner.
My Mummy sings to me
at bedtinne.

I Love Mum.

*Figure 63*

My teacher is very lively and is alway busy. She moves about like Roadrunner. She teaches us dance and every other class in the School. We have been doing Chinese movements and they are slow and calm. Our teacher can move so slowly and softly. We all pretended to be gentle hovering birds. Mrs D also teaches us other subjects, maths, english, history, Science, art. We always do our beginnings of lessons sitting on the Carpet around her. She sits very still and talks to us calmly but if the topic is exciting She jumps about a lot again. Sometimes She is angry when people are naughty and She looks very cross. She bends her body over who she's really telling off but mostly She is happy. She smiles a lot and if Something is funny She laughs.

*Figure 64*

## Looking at child-to-child interaction

Movement information can be used to advantage in supporting and enriching child-to-child interaction and communication. So often, it is the secure and confident children who are 'given' the new and diffident ones to look after. The quick reactors are asked to help those who come along slowly. When left to their own devices to whom do children most easily relate? They may communicate at first with just one or two children. Is there anything common to be found in terms of movement expression among those who habitually congregate together? Is there anything common in those children who are less often approached or included?

It may be a useful exercise, once in a while, to look at the movement characteristics shared, or not shared, in this way. This is not to encourage any sort of in-grouping or elitism, or to negate the fact that social development implies growing abilities to let go of self and relate to others. But, if the expressive qualities of the children are well known to the adult involved in caring and educating them, it should be possible to facilitate 'sharing', 'looking after', and 'motivating' roles from time to time, as well as to encourage mixing and socialising in less familiar movement-shared relationships.

# SUMMARY

At the beginning of this chapter the point was made that movement does not tell us everything we need to know about each other. That remains true but there are times when movement can say more than words. On such occasions we should have the confidence to trust our feelings. In response to the movement cues which our children give us, a restraining hand, a fierce embrace, a hug, an encouraging nod, a shared smile may be all that is needed. If this is the case we should let it happen that way and then proceed from there.

# 7 Dance, Dance, Wherever You May Be

## Where does dance belong?

Throughout the past two decades, debate has increasingly centred on the appropriate 'placing' of dance. Where does it rightfully belong? There are those who claim that, because of the movement basis of dance, it belongs, as it has done for so many years, to physical education. Others, a growing number, argue that it is an art form alongside music, art and drama with which it has strong, generic links. The long and heated debate has, for the present, been decided for us – by the government. Within the National Curriculum, dance takes its place along with the other activities within the statutory order for physical education.

*Figure 65    Dancing is a special sort of movement    Photo © Catherine Ashmore*

Perhaps for young children up to the age of eight years it matters less where it takes its place than for older children. The early childhood educators have less in the way of formalised subject categories to restrict them and cross-curricular links emerge naturally for children and adults alike. It is only at a later stage, when dance, and teachers of dance, become more specialised, that the debate of where dance belongs becomes significant. But while academic and philosophical debate proceeds the children continue to dance, come what may, and adults continue to support them wherever it occurs and in whatever ways are most appropriate.

All dance is movement but not all movement is dance. While sharing a movement base with other activities, Flemming (1974, p. 5) describes dance as having something extra:

> *the added dimension of aesthetic, creative*
> *and inner self expression which is so*
> *important in young children's lives.*

## PERFORMING, CREATING AND VIEWING DANCE

We turn now to the ways in which young children engage in dance as they take on 'roles' of performer, creator and viewer. It is important to stress here that no attempt is made to provide programmes of study or lesson plans although reference will be made to these, from time to time. There are several recent books on dance which give excellent guidance on structure and content at different stages of learning and which readers might be interested to consult, for example Harlow and Rolfe (1992), Gough (1993), and Harrison (1993).

The triumvirate of creating, performing and appreciating dance as a conceptual basis underlying all phases of dance education (see figure 66) was first put forward by Smith (1988, p. 258). Until that time, the so-called child-centred approach, stemming from the ideas of Laban, and the professional model, influenced by the professional world of dance, existed as separate, and often opposing, entities. The second of these featured mainly in secondary and higher education while the first remained in the domain of primary education. Smith (now Smith Autard) has continued to act as a significant leader in the field of dance education and her merging of the 'educational' and 'professional' models has received much acclaim. However, the assimilation of her ideas have, until recently and with notable exceptions, been more effectively and relevantly realised in secondary rather than primary education. Although the model itself has become firmly established, Davies (1994 p. 73) points out:

*the ways in which the notions and concepts within these areas can be applied to different cultures, styles and client groups are still relatively new. It is the relevant and appropriate application of the model which is the important issue now.*

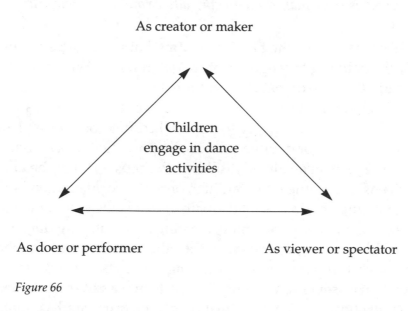

Figure 66

## Identifying the nature of provision for the very young

It is with this realisation that we turn now to children within the first phase of living and look at what the three established 'roles' mean in their lives and the lives of those who take responsibility for their learning. In marrying the 'educational' and 'professional' models it is important to ensure that what takes place at secondary level is not simply watered down to cater for the younger children. The performance, creative and appreciation components now firmly in place in secondary education are there in a different form in the dance of young children. But we need to take care to start from their own abilities and interests.

There is no reason why the dance activity of the very young should not happen in similar ways to the other arts and yet that doesn't always seem to be so. In making a case for dance in the home, nursery or school, to be catered for in a similar way to music and literature and with reference to the inter-dependent activities of doing, making and viewing, Davies (1988, p. 741) writes:

*In these areas children are not just restricted to making their own sound
compositions or making up their own stories. As well as being young writers or
young composers they listen to music by established composers and on most days
of the week listen to a story read by their parents, carers, teachers and peers. In
doing so they become appreciators. When they tell or read their own stories or play
their own sound compositions they become performers with friends as a live
audience always more than ready to offer advice and to become critic of the day.*

Why are composing, performing and spectating happening less readily in dance
then in music or painting or language or model making? Why does dance feature
less prominently than the other arts? Perhaps it is because dance means more in
terms of organisation and therefore acts as a deterrent. Clearing a space, gathering
children together, making a journey to a special corner, room or hall and, in the
case of children in infant and junior schools, helping them to get changed, can
seem like major events in an already full day. Perhaps it is that the language of
dance itself needs to become more familiar, or that information on how to
introduce it to young children is inadequate. If this is the case it may help to look
now in some detail at how performing, creating and watching dance can happen
with young children. Comparisons with the other arts can then be made.

    With young children the three identifying concepts are necessarily flexible
structures and carry several meanings. To perform can at times be taken to
mean 'to do', 'to show' 'to dance'. Creating can be translated as 'making' or
'composing' while appreciation encapsulates 'watching' and 'viewing' dance.

## THE CHILD AS PERFORMER

For the very young this may simply mean dancing. In this instance the term
'performance' gets its meaning from those who are watching rather than from
any performance aspirations on the part of the children dancing. For slightly
older children it may signify dancing 'to' or 'for' another person, or a particular
event. This entails the children 'showing' what they can do. Alternatively,
showing may take place as part of sharing experiences. The showing is the nonverbal counterpart of telling. It should not be confused with 'showing off' with
its attendant 'exhibiting' characteristics although a little of this may legitimately
be present. For the two- and three-year-olds the performing role is often
associated with dancing with those around them. 'Come and dance with me' is
a frequently heard invitation. It is also one which can be given, in turn, by
adults to individuals or groups of children.

Young children carry their performance space around with them. It is the space where a dance is danced for the first time or where it is repeated. It is thoroughly portable: it can travel anywhere, the number of 'showings' depending on the depth and extent of interest. It may first be presented to mother at home in the kitchen or to the nursery staff in the home corner; then in the garden to brothers and sisters on their arrival home from school; and, later, to father in the living room before it is time for bed.

At an earlier age than might first be imagined performance is seen as something more than dancing. The idea of 'performance' is extended to incorporate a sense of venue. Almost every day, Kathryn chose a tutu from the dressing-up clothes, put on the cassette player and danced to the music. There was something over and above the personal love of dancing which was strongly present. This 'something' was an extra sense of performance seen in the way in which she prepared the dancing area and responded to the children and nursery staff who often stopped by to share the 'event'. Kathyrn attended ballet lessons twice a week and was already showing exceptional 'danceability'. She was absorbed in her dancing and her dancing absorbed her. 'Preschool dance is concerned with sensory awareness of movement and deep involvement in the movement' (Stinson, 1988, p. 4).

## Performance at School

### Dance and 'skill'

Once into the infant school children enter a situation where performing, taking its place alongside creating and viewing, becomes an important and well-articulated part of dance education. Harlow and Rolfe (1992, p. 15) advise that equal attention must be given to the three clearly identified strands. However, within this general rule the nature and relative amounts of each strand will vary according to the age and experience of the children. Whenever the subject of performance in relation to young children is raised, inevitably so is the subject of skill. There are many and varied views on this issue. Williams (1988, p. 28) draws our attention to children as performers being a dangerous aim of dance education unless it is fully understood. She warns that some teachers have pre-conceived models and directly instruct the class in order for the children to achieve the necessary standards. She argues:

*Dance is a performing art but it is erroneously considered that the degree of technical skill must be reasonably high before children can be engaged in the art form of the subject.*

This view appears, at first, to be countered by Harlow and Rolfe (1992, p. 15) who claim:

*The mastery of basic skills is essential to enable them to move with ease and precision, allowing them to release their individuality in imaginative situations.*

The authors go on, however, to suggest that mastery of basic skills refers here to an expanding dance vocabulary rather than acquisition of particular bodily skills. Initially, they suggest, teaching should concentrate on bodily, dynamic and spatial aspects of movement. There is no doubt that the eloquence of performance reflects both the personal expressive characteristics of the children and the progressive development of these through an appropriate set of experiences.

## Planned performance

Once children start at infant school the activity of sharing, which inevitably has something of a sense of performance about it, is different. Performance is now two-fold and intentionally planned. First, it continues as a participatory activity in response to suggestions, for example, to:

- move freely to the music; or

- creep, crawl, wriggle and flop.

In response to both challenges the children move in concert with each other. In moving freely to the music, a range of different instruments (the children's bodies) play different tunes (their movement phrases). In creeping, crawling, wriggling and flopping, different instruments (the children's bodies) play the same tune (the movement phrase) but with individual, personal qualities. Figure 67 shows Richard, aged six, creeping. We can see the cautious way he advances from the restrained expression of his body. Notice how he puts only the outside of his right foot on the floor as he steps, indicating being quiet and careful.

*Figure 67    Advancing with slow, careful movement*

The second aspect of performance in the infant and junior schools is that the children are now asked, from time to time, to demonstrate how they have responded to the challenges which were set. For example, the teacher might say:

> *Let us all watch Shalom and notice especially how he seems to soar through the air and the soft way he melts into the floor as his dance ends.*

As Shalom listens to the teacher's guidelines given to the class he receives clues about what is expected from his performance. It is a way of reminding him of what he is to do as well as focusing the attention of the those watching. As a result of this his 'thinking body' becomes focused and he is able to give fully of himself. These are two important attributes of performance.

## Performing for other people

Both in and out of school children show their dances to each other. Sometimes they show them to another class, or to the whole school, perhaps at a school assembly or during a time which is set aside for sharing. Occasionally, children show their dance to parents and friends at a special event.

When the performance space changes from the hall or classroom to a stage or some other 'theatre space' yet another level of performance consciousness is reached and a different sort of excitement is felt. When handled well, such occasions are exciting, enriching experiences where children's dance is seen within a supportive and informative setting. The audience needs to know what is involved and how to look in order to understand and respond. The children's dance requires the same serious attention as that given to any of the other art forms in which they express their ideas and feelings. When the 'programme' represents the children's own work and is seen as an illustration of their artistic and aesthetic development there is little danger of inappropriate responses from the audience. It is only when children appear as instruments of adult conceptions, such as in some Nativity plays where they attempt shepherd's dances and the like, that it can go wrong. The 'ohs' 'ahs' and generous smiles of those who watch, help to make such performances a spectacle. Lowden (1989, p. 71) puts a similar warning this way:

> . . . consider the kind of sharing that happens, say, at Christmas. At the most limited level of sharing parents come to admire their children and apart from parental pride, the criteria for spectating are those of stage and screen cut down.

Writing specifically in relation to children under five years, Stinson (1988, p. 8) suggests that making a 'show for parents is almost always doomed to failure'. However as the children progress in their understanding of themselves and of dance this is not necessarily the case and many such performances inform the audience and delight the children.

Boorman (1991, p. 18) makes a case for the education of parents and 'significant adults' so that they come to know and appreciate their children in this special kind of setting. She advises:

> We have to ensure that adults recognize that children's art has to be more than mere entertainment; it has to go beyond the 'cute' and become evocation and response between child and adult: a mutual giving and receiving.

## THE CHILD AS COMPOSER

Performing and composing are often inextricably mixed. This is particularly so for young children whose dance is dancing and dancing is the dance. There is no magic formula which brings forth a dance-maker, or choreographer, at a particular age. There is no special moment when the mantle of choreographer is assumed. It is an activity which is built up gradually, and through a diversity of experiences, from an early age.

## Making dance statements, phrases and dances

This, arguably, is one of the most common objectives in helping children develop personal and interpersonal creativity in dance. It provides a broad framework which can be adapted as situations demand but, in essence, is concerned with appropriate structuring devices which can be used for developing dance creativity in young children. There are important questions to be asked and answered. What are these structuring devices? Do they facilitate or restrict? How should they be used? Should they be used at all with young children?

We are not, of course, starting from scratch. There is plenty of evidence to suggest that the creative process is already in operation from a very early age. Sometimes it is the rhythm of what young children do which is all-important. Sometimes the patterns they make are absorbing, while at other times they are caught up in what their bodies can achieve or how it feels to be dancing with someone else. Children's movement is often full of contrast – at one time gentle and calm, at another fierce and stormy, for example as it sweeps through the space, makes a bid for the sky and literally collides with the earth. It is a canvas of dance activity such as this which the children bring to their child-minders, their grandparents, to their nursery, infant and junior schools. It is a canvas which provides convincing evidence for the *raison d'etre* of dance education. Harlow and Rolfe (1992, p. 16) write:

> *It is the aim of dance education in the early years to foster and develop all these natural abilities by providing opportunities for pupils to create or compose simple dance sequences . . .*

There are several structuring devices which can be used effectively with children between three and eight years. Three examples are given below.

### Linking
One important choreographic device is the transition from one movement idea to another – the way in which movement ideas and activities are linked. Perhaps the simplest illustration of this, and one which allows the maximum

choice for children, deals with opposites. For example, making a short 'quick and slow dance' in response to some sort of accompaniment. This requires the children to make two appropriate selections of movement (one for the slow part and another for the quick part) and to incorporate a changeover time. In this case the ideas to be linked are well known opposites set to a simple accompaniment. Eventually, like a home-made song, the children dance it again and again. Then, at the end of the day, it can be shown to family and friends in the same way as their paintings, stories, and models. Unlike the paintings, stories and models, however, it is lost as soon as it ceases to be danced. The transitory nature of dance makes it difficult to keep on-going written records but perhaps this difficulty could to a certain extent be overcome if childhood educators could keep photographic records or, better still, video scrapbooks of the children's work.

Here is another, more complex, example of linking. It involves a tambour being played for the children in the following ways:

- beating the tambour with a beater;

- tapping the rim of the tambour with the end of the beater;

- drawing the finger nails across the skin of the tambour.

The different sounds which emerge are first explored separately as the children respond in their own ways to what they hear. The sound patterns are then put in a set sequence for the children to create their 'tambour dances'. As well as the structure set for them by the order in which the different sounds appear, the children are able to see the changes being made – which end of the beater is being used, or when the finger nails take over. Seeing, as well as hearing, is especially helpful for three- and four-year-olds in their initial attempts to structure experiences of this kind.

Linking continues as a transitional technique through all phases of dance education and is also seen in a variety of professional choreography.

## Association

Certain movement ideas seem to belong together: running and leaping; turning and twisting; landing and rolling; running swiftly; landing gently; spinning freely; straight and narrow; zigzag and spiky; curved and soft. Exploration of these phrases which seem to have a natural kinship brings about a differentiation of rhythm in each case and an accompanying sense of mastery.

### External structures

As well as natural devices such as linking and association, reference to external structures can help to give dances form. Such structures can be natural or man-made. In the firework dance, considered at some length on pages 108–10, the three phases of firework activity provided the structure. In a similar way the seasons – spring, summer, autumn and winter – are natural phenomena which can be used for structuring dance activity. Winter, for example, conjures up many movement images (being blown by a cold wind and alternately freezing and melting) and lends itself well to dance. Here again, the sequence of events influences the structure of the dance although such order does not necessarily have to be adhered to. Just as there is poetic licence so too there is dance licence – both in early childhood and at professional level. In her volcano dance, six-year-old Leah expressed the melting of lava. She had lovely control of her body as she sank into the ground and she chose a sustained, flexible quality of movement to show how lava meanders slowly along its path.

## Dances can't be made from nothing

Clearly, dance-making needs to have substance. It cannot exist in a void. Just as poetry needs words and sculpture requires substances like clay or wood, so dance composition needs movement to give it shape and form. As children become more and more familiar with the building blocks of dance – the material of movement – they begin slowly to differentiate between the process and the product. Unless they achieve familiarity with a wide range of movement possibilities, creativity cannot effectively take place. Instead, children will be seen to produce the same movements and movement patterns time and time again. Petricevia (*daCi International Proceedings*, 1988, p. 253) puts it this way:

> *Children's imagination accepts no limits of expression but creativity is hindered by an inarticulate movement vocabulary.*

In addition to a rich and varied movement vocabulary, a range of sources and resources play an important part in the creative process. Ideas and stimuli can trigger off a whole spectrum of dance images which result in dance play, dance sequences and whole dances. Apart from movement – the first and most readily available source of inspiration – there are many sources which help children to structure their dances. Within the confines of this book it is only possible to consider a few of these – and these only briefly.

## Sound

Self-expressed sound and movement make for interesting dance. The 'whoo' sound which elongates and shortens melodically and dynamically as a plane takes off, twists, turns and lands is a good example (figure 68). It is a common favourite expressed by individual children many times over and reflects the ways in which young children naturally accompany their movement.

## Action words

The human voice is an immediately available source used by adults to stimulate dance responses. Brief references in Chapter 5 drew attention to the need for the teacher to match the quality of vocal sound to the content of the phrase.

Action words and phrases can enhance or extend actions which children have in their repertoire but only if spoken with articulate relevance. Children love to make up their own phrases. A favourite activity of six-, seven- and eight-year-olds is to accompany each other's dances. Even more fun is to swap action phrases with each other. One child's action phrase 'creep, crawl, pounce and catch' contrasts quite strongly with another's 'running, jumping and rolling along'. The 'action swap shop' is a fun way for children to get on the inside of

*Figure 68    The body tilts and the wings regulate as the plane turns*

each other's dance and, in doing so, to extend their own movement vocabulary and sense of phrasing.

## Poetry

Sometimes a short poem is a good starting point. Two elements are important here. First, the poem should possess a good helping of movement ideas and not be totally descriptive. Second, it must be well spoken or read. This poem by Eleanor Farjeon, 'The Tide in the River', is particularly suitable in length and content for younger children of three to five years.

> *The tide in the river,*
> *The tide in the river,*
> *The tide in the river runs deep,*
> *I saw a shiver*
> *Pass over the river*
> *As the tide turns in its sleep.*

The poem can be used in a variety of ways. One of these would be to take the three activities without the words and work with the children as follows:

- travelling smoothly and with change of level – going from high to low;

- travelling smoothly, introducing a shiver which goes through the whole body;

- making a big, slow, turning movement.

When the children have had time to make these activities their own, they may then be ready to perform them in accompaniment to the words. Using the poem in this way means that demands are not so exacting as to cause difficulties for the younger children and the framework provides a security which is not too rigorous.

## Percussion

Percussion instruments are fun as a source for dance. They can be used to stimulate, to accompany, or both. The range of sound which can be produced varies with the instrument. Different too are the responses to the sounds as we saw in the tambour dances (p. 148). In providing the percussive stimulus the 'accompanist' can control, to a certain extent, the dynamics and shape of the phrase and has the freedom to modify it accordingly. When children handle percussion for their own dances they shape their own phrasing.

## Recorded music

Music is an established partner for dance and, perhaps, the most familiar one. It can provide rhythmic vitality, simple phrasing and lyrical or dramatic backcloths or atmospheres. But there needs to be some safeguards relating to its use. With the youngest children aged between two and four years it is probably best to use it sparingly and in a highly selective way for, as Davies (Brearley ed. 1969, p. 80) reminds us:

> Children in the early years are busy establishing their own rhythms and most find it difficult to conform to highly structured patterns not of their own making.

This does not mean that music should not be used at all but rather that selection should be carefully considered. There are three major ways in which it might be used for young children's dance:

- for improvisation and free response;

- for the introduction and deepening of specific dance ideas;

- for observation and follow-up of children's spontaneous activity.

In the first of these a record is played and the children respond without intervention of any kind. Such occasions give the children an opportunity to dance freely without restrictions other than the music. They illustrate the learning phase of exploration discussed on page 84. The second concentrates on enriching and extending specific movement ideas which are currently being explored. The third use of recorded music is to support the children's own dancing – to provide an appropriate backcloth against which their movement can take place.

## Touch

In their active exploration of the environment children are constantly touching and handling things. Touch often brings with it an almost instantaneous expressive quality of movement. Banging fists on the table, stroking the cat or the feel of dry sand running through fingers are just a few of the experiences involving touch which happen during the day. Many of these experiences can be utilised in the context of dance. One way of doing this is through linking the dance to the original action, for example, taking the stroking action of the palms and enlarging it to involve the whole arm or two arms moving together. Strokes can be taken into different areas in space – in front, to the side and behind the body. Stroking can be done with extreme gentleness and contrasted with a strong and energetic banging action.

## Clothes

It is well known that we are influenced by what we wear. And that what we wear influences how we move. High heels and tight skirts bring about a different sort of self-presentation from jeans and a baggy sweater. The same applies to dance. The size, shape, and weight of dressing-up materials all influence dance-making. They often set it off. Many a witch dance has arisen from a long, black cloak, the same cloak which, on other occasions, has symbolised king-like qualities. Baggy trousers may suggest clowns or pirates, white scarves the clouds or snow.

## The environment

The environment, both natural and man-made, is rich in providing ideas for dance. The actions and moods of the sea, the fish and plants which inhabit it, and the sand and rocks on which it breaks, are full of dance images. So too is the much talked-about British weather and the seasons with which it is naturally, or sometimes unnaturally, associated. Lots of action and qualities of movement stem from the observation of animals: cats that pounce, frogs and kangeroos that jump and snakes that slither and slide. Whirligigs drying the clothes, mechanical toys, swings and roundabouts are all movement-invested happenings with which children – and adults – are familiar and which, along with numerous other phenomena, provide good starting points for dance.

# THE CHILD AS SPECTATOR

This part of the three-pronged model has, to some extent, been looked at already. In essence, it is the counterpart of performing or showing. Sharing dances with, or performing dances to, friends and peers is a reciprocal process. One minute children are performers, the next minute they are a member – sometimes the only member – of an audience. There surely can be no better way than this of coming to 'know' the art of dance. For in the early years of childhood, there is no sense that some can 'do' and others 'only watch', an attitude which, regrettably, sometimes creeps in later on. Because watching is an integral part of the total dance education scenario it has a meaning and a value of its own. And, because the language of dance is a common one, the basis for watching and recognising is already in place. In examining the relationship between learning through participation in dance and learning about dance, Killingbeck (1993, p. 4) suggests that:

> *Participation in dance activity makes a unique contribution to a child's aesthetic appreciation of dance as art, and that practical experience fundamentally underpins and is a necessary condition for the development of an aesthetic appreciation of dance as art in education.*

The appreciation element, thought by some to be missing from dance education of the 1960s and 1970s, has always been there in the learning of young children where 'doing and viewing' are considered as interchangable partners. These dance activities fit well into the general practice of early childhood education where looking, listening and commenting have always taken their place as important ingredients of learning.

'Spectating', 'viewing', 'appreciating', or whatever name is given to this activity, is a progressive affair. Eventually, 'authentic' language is necessary for children, even young children, to fulfil the role. Progression from the two-year-old through to the eight-year-old comes about through the ability to carry out, and more importantly, to relate some of the following spectator activities:

- identifying;
- naming;
- describing;
- commenting upon;
- reflecting upon;
- critically appraising.

The first remarks of parents and carers to their children as they dance are important. 'What a lovely stretch your body has', 'You are almost flying through the air' and 'That position is really strong' are early comments which help to build the foundation on which dance viewing and the later stage of appreciation are built. The subsequent succession of people who take on the care and education of young children need to continue to comment in this fashion as they support and enrich the children's dance experience. And, at an appropriate time, they need to share the responsibility for increasingly informed comment with both individual children and small groups. At six, seven and eight years that responsibility can be transferred more and more to the children who are gradually able to shape their own critical dialogue.

## The Legend of Panku

A class of seven- and eight-year-olds in a primary school in the Midlands are used to making, performing and commenting on their dances. They recently made up and performed a dance based on the legend of Panku. Here is how Suzanne and Gregory, both seven, describe what happened.

Suzanne says:

_Making our dance_

Our dance was based on a Chinese legend. We thought about how Chinese people moved in their long dresses. We did little tiny steps and put our hands together with our elbows out to enter. All our positions were balanced, so we looked calm.

I helped to make up the wind section. We did gentle swirls and turns. We were so soft we did the movement on our own and then joined together to make a cloud that bounced softly and gently in the sky. We turned and turned so gently, then softly creeping we made our way back to our places. I like the movement we made up.

*Figure 69*

And Gregory describes it like this:

> **Performing** the dance Party
> Yesterday we did our Chinese legend for the
> first time infront of an audience I was nervous
> and I was glad we did things altogether
> to begin with. When it came my turn to be the
> Thunder I really enjoyed it. I jumped high and
> put lots of energy into my dance I did not look at
> the audience I just thought of the dance.
> The space seemed much smaller than in our
> practices but we were careful not to bump
> into eachother. At the end I thought it was ace
> and I can't wait to do it for my mum and
> dad next week.

*Figure 70*

It is interesting for us to note here the different emphasis the children give in their descriptions. Suzanne calls hers 'Making our dance' while Gregory names his 'Performing the dance'. Their comments also show the attention given by Suzanne to telling us what the dance was about while Gregory found the element of performance and sharing exciting. Unless the children had articulated their responses to this experience we would not have so fully appreciated the different reactions they had.

We also learn something of the dance from figure 71 showing Timothy, aged seven, who was part of the sun group. He is able to make his body, his costume and the piece of material he handles a meaningful whole as he expresses his ideas of the sun. He moves with confidence and understanding.

*Figure 71    Timothy's sun dance*

## Widening the image of dance

The child's role in viewing dance is helped by contact with the professional world. A very simple and natural way of doing this is through the medium of television and video. Just as children may watch football, rugby, gardening, or cookery specialists with the rest of the family, so too can they become aware of the professional dancers and dance-makers who appear on our screens from time to time. These include artists not only from contemporary and classical dance genres but also those from a wide variety of different cultures.

The work of educational units, attached to professional companies, have much to offer to children in infant and junior schools. The nature of their involvement varies from company to company but professional dancers are usually included in the team which visits the school. Sometimes the visit lasts only half a day but for older children the 'residency' might go on for a week and may also be shared with another school. Such a visit or residency can be a rare and exciting treat when children see, and even dance with, 'real dancers' and attend live performances.

## For those children with a special interest in dance

The more young children get interested in things the more they want to do. We looked earlier at children's needs to conquer traditional skills such as skipping and catching. Thirsts of this kind also apply to the pursuit of favourite categories of interest. Some children have special interests in computers, others in drama, games, or poetry. Similarly, some children are 'into dance' and can't get enough of it. Writing about the development of interests, Katz (1991, p. 30) makes this point:

> *An important disposition of concern to educators of young children is interest, or the capacity 'to lose' in an activity or concern outside of oneself. Interest refers to the capability of becoming deeply enough absorbed in something to pursue it over time, with sufficient commitment to accept the routine as well as novel aspects of work.*

While such enthusiasm is natural enough for children, it often poses problems for parents. Should their children enter a situation which may be less flexible than they would like, involve the acquisition of adult skills, mean making a journey, cost money? The questions and self-addressed answers in each case will vary according to philosophy, family priorities and economics. However, it could reasonably be argued that there is now much greater choice about dance opportunities than ever before. Local dance schools, where ballet, tap and modern styles are taught, abound. There are opportunities, too, for children to take part in the dance of other cultures such as Asian, Irish or Greek. South Indian dance is renowned for its dramatic expression using the face and the hands. In figure 72, Bavaani Nanthabalan from the Academy of Indian Dance shows young children the hand gesture, or mudra, for 'the deer' as part of a story-telling workshop.

Costs apart, the question of whether or not young children should be taught set patterns of movement remains debatable. For some it may not be appropriate. But, for others, who find no stress but only enjoyment in such a situation, and gain individual satisfaction within the set parameters, there is perhaps less to fear.

Increasingly, local education authorities are setting up and supporting youth dance groups and these, in turn, are opening their doors to younger members. While mostly dancing within their own age groups they also participate with children of different ages. Costs of youth groups of this kind are normally minimal, the method of teaching educationally appropriate, and creative

Figure 72    A story-telling workshop

workshops a high priority. Dance companies, through their education and community units, provide workshops and classes of different kinds as well as introducing children to the dances and dancers of the professional theatre.

Into whatever category dance opportunities of this sort might fall, and whatever problems there might seem to be, there are also benefits. The children will be dancing with a group of like-minded enthusiasts, all of whom have chosen to do so. It gives additional scope for the children's dance vocabulary to be widened and for them to be involved in making dances and performing dances with a particular group of people. The children become generally more educated in dance. The non-dance bonuses go without saying as children gain confidence, build up a sense of belonging, make friends, anticipate and reflect on what is important at any particular time.

Although widening experience in this way is of value to all children, it is of special significance to children whose intense interest incorporates signs of special ability. We sometimes need reminding that children with an element of 'giftedness' require a measure of special provision just as much as those children with learning difficulties.

## Summary

Dance, as experienced by young children as makers, doers and spectators, necessarily has some things in common with professional dance but it needs always to be understood and conducted in relation to a sound educational framework.

Bringing us full circle, and connecting the world of the child with the world of professional dance, Judith Jamison, an American contemporary dancer, writes:

> There's only one of me. There's only one of anybody. That's why steps look different on different people.

## Helping Children to Learn Through a Movement Perspective: Towards The Future

Movement matters. Most adults know this and make great efforts to support their children in the activities of their choice. We are on the way to a stage where movement is accepted as an essential part of early childhood education and regarded as a respectable and respected contribution to the learning process.

What is needed now are two things. One, for practitioners world-wide to share their practice, the observations they make, and the records they keep of the children's learning through a movement perspective. And, two, for researchers and theorists world-wide to use these as they look into the underpinning on which good practice is based. When this dialogue occurs on a regular and systematic basis movement will most certainly take its rightful place within an early childhood context and 'movement be seen to matter'.

# BIBLIOGRAPHY

ACGB, (1993) *Dance in Schools*. London: ACGB.

Adshead, J. (1981) *The Study of Dance*. London: Dance Books.

Alexander, R. J. (1988) *Primary Teaching*. London: Cassell Educational Ltd.

Almond, L. (1989) *The Place of Physical Education in Schools*. London: Kegan Paul.

*A Puffin Quartet of Poets* (1958) Harmondsworth: Penguin Books Ltd.

Argyle, M. and Trower, P. (1979) *Person to Person: Ways of Communication*. London: Harper & Row Ltd.

Armstrong, N. (ed.) (1992) *New Directions in Physical Education Volume 2: Towards a National Curriculum*. Leeds: Human Kinetics Publishers (Europe) Ltd.

Arnold, P.J. (1979) *Meaning in Movement, Sport and Physical Education*. London: Heinemann Educational Books Ltd.

Arnold, P.J. (1988) *Education, Movement and the Curriculum*. London: The Falmer Press.

Athey, C. (1990) *Extending Thought in Young Children: A Parent-Teacher Partnership*. London: Paul Hamlyn.

Ball, C. (1994) *Start Right: The Importance of Early Learning*. London: RSA.

Bartenieff, I. with Lewis, D. (1980) *Body Movement: Coping With the Environment*. London: Gordon & Breach Science Publishers.

Bartholomew, L. and Bruce, T. (1993) *Getting To Know You: A guide to record-keeping in early childhood education and care*. London: Hodder & Stoughton.

Bee, H. (1992) *The Developing Child*. New York: Harper Collins College Publishers.

Blenkin, G. and Kelly, A. (1987) *Early Childhood Education*. London: Paul Chapman Publishing Company.

Boorman, J. (1969) *Creative Dance in the First Three Grades*. Canada: Longmans Canada Limited.

Boorman, P. (1987) 'The Contributions of Physical Activity to Development in the Early Years'. In *Early Childhood Education*, G. Blenkin and V. Kelly (eds). London: Paul Chapman.

Borton, H. (1963) *Do You Move As I Do?* London: Abelard-Schuman.

Brearley, M. (ed.) (1969) *Fundamentals in the First School*. Oxford: Blackwell.

Bredekamp, S. (ed.) (1987) *Developmentally Appropriate Practice in Early Childhood Programs Serving From Birth Through Age 8*. Washington: NAEYC.

Brierley, J. (1987) *Give Me a Child Until He is Seven*. London: The Falmer Press.

Brown, D. (1994) 'Play, the Playground and the Culture of Children'. In *The Excellence of Play*, J. Moyles (ed.). Milton Keynes OUP.

Bruce, T. (1987) *Early Childhood Education*. London: Hodder & Stoughton.

Bruce, T. (1988) 'The Implications of the National Curriculum for Early Childhood Education'. TACTYC Journal 9, Number 1.

Bruce, T. (1991) *Time to Play in Early Childhood Education*. London: Hodder & Stoughton.

Bruner, J. (1968) *Towards a Theory of Instruction*. Cambridge, MA: Harvard University Press.

Bruner, J. (1974) *Beyond the Imagination Given*. London: Allen & Unwin.

Bruner, J. (1985) *Child's Talk*. London: W.W. Norton & Company Inc.

Churcher, B. (1971) *Physical Education for Teaching*. London: George Allen and Unwin Ltd.

David, T. (1990) *Under Five: Under Educated?* Milton Keynes: OUP.

Davies, M. (1969) 'Action, Feeling and Thought'. In *Fundamentals in the First School*, M. Brearley (ed.). Oxford: Blackwell.

Davies, M. (1976) 'An Investigation into Movement Related to Some Aspects of Cognitive Development in Young Children'. (Unpublished PhD thesis. University of London.)

Davies, M. (1989) 'Of Secondary Importance and Primary Concern: Prioritising the Study of Dance'. In *4th daCi International Conference Proceedings*. London: daCi UK.

Davies, M. (1994) Good Practice in Dance. In *Dance Matters*. London: NDTA.

Department of Education and Science (1989) *Aspects of Primary Education: The Education of Children Under Five*. London: HMSO.

Department of Education and Science (1990) *Starting With Quality: The Report of Inquiry into the Quality of the Educational Experience Offered to 3 and 4 Year Olds*. London: HMSO.

Department of Education and Science (1992) *Physical Education in the National Curriculum*. London: HMSO.

Donaldson, M. (1978) *Children's Minds*. London: Fontana.

Drummond, M.J. (1993) *Assessing Children's Learning*. London: David Fulton Press.

EYGC (1989) *Early Childhood Education: The Early Years Curriculum and the National Curriculum*. Stoke on Trent: Trentham Books.

Fantz, R.L. (1961) 'The Origin of Form Perception'. In *Scientific American* (no. 459).

Flemming, G. (1973) *Children's Dance*. Washington: American Association for Health, Physical Education and Recreation.

Floyd, A. (ed.) (1979) *Cognitive Development in the School Years*. London: Croom Helm.

Gallahue, D. (1982) *Developmental Experiences for Children*. New York: MacMillan Publishing Company.

Gallahue, D. (1989) *Understanding Motor Development: Infants, Children, Adolescents*. Dubuque: Brown and Benchmark (printers).

Gentle, K. (1985) *Children and Art Teaching*. London: Croom Helm.

Gerhardt, L. (1973) *Moving and Knowing: The Young Child Orients Himself in Space*. New Jersey: Prentice-Hall Inc.

Ginsburg, H. and Opper, S. (1969) *Piaget's Theory of Intellectual Development*. New Jersey: Prentice-Hall Inc.

Groves, L. (1989) 'Children With Special Needs' In *Issues in Physical Education for the Primary Years*, A. Williams (ed.). Lewes: The Falmer Press.

Gura, P. (ed.) (1992) *Exploring Learning: Young Children and Blockplay*. London: Paul Chapman Publishing Ltd.

Hampson, S.E. (1982) *The Construction of Personality*. London: Routledge & Kegan Paul Ltd.

Harlow, M. and Rolfe, L. (1992) *Let's Dance: A Handbook for Teachers*. London: BBC Educational Publishing.

Harrison, K. (1993) *Let's Dance*. London: Hodder & Stoughton.

Hurst, V. (1991) *Planning for Early Learning: Education in the First Five Years*. London: Paul Chapman Publishing Ltd.

Hurst, V. (1994) 'Observing Play in Early Childhood'. In *The Excellence of Play*, Moyles (ed.). Milton Keynes: OUP

Hutt, J.S., Tyler, S., Hutt, C. and Christopherson, H. (1988) *Play, Exploration and Learning: A Natural History of the Pre-school*. London: Routledge.

Ives, S.W. (1984) 'The development of expressivity in drawing'. In *The British Journal of Educational Psychology* Vol. 54, pp. 152–9.

Jackson, L. (1993) *Childsplay: Movement Games for Fun and Fitness*. London: Thorsons.

Laban, R. (1948) *Modern Educational Dance*. London: MacDonald & Evans.

Laban, R. (1960) *The Mastery of Movement*. London: MacDonald & Evans.

Laban, R. (1966) *Choreutics*. London: MacDonald & Evans.

Laban, R. (1980) *The Mastery of Movement*. London: MacDonald & Evans.

Laban, R. and Lawrence, F. (1947) *Effort*. London: MacDonald & Evans.

Lamb, W. (1965) *Posture and Gesture*. London: Gerald Duckworth & Co. Ltd.

Lamb, W. and Watson, E. (1979) *Body Code: The Meaning in Movement*. London: Routledge & Kegan Paul.

Lovell, M. (1976) *Your Growing Child*. London: Routledge & Kegan Paul.

Katz, L. (ed.) (1977) *Current Topics in Education* Volume I. New Jersey: Ablex Publishing Corporation.

Lally, M. (1991) *The Nursery Teacher in Action*. London: Paul Chapman Publishing Ltd.

Maletic, V. (1987) *Body-Space-Expression: The Development of Rudolf Laban's Movement and Dance Concepts*. Berlin: Walter de Gruyter & Co.

Matthews, J. (1988) 'The Young Child's Representation and Drawing'. In *Early Childhood Education: A Developmental Curriculum*, G. Blenkin and V. Kelly (eds.). London: Paul Chapman Publishing Ltd.

Matthews, J. (1995) *Helping Children to Draw and Paint in Early Childhood*. London: Hodder & Stoughton.

Meadows, S. (1993) *The Child As Thinker: The Development and Acquisition of Cognition in Childhood*. London: Routledge.

Meadows, S. and Cashdan, A. (1988) *Helping Children Learn*. London: David Fulton Publishers.

McPherson, B.D., Curtis, J.E. and Loy, J.W. (1989) *The Social Significance of Sport*. Illinois: Human Kinetics Books

Moyles, J. (1989) *Just Playing: The Role and Status of Play in Early Childhood Education*. Milton Keynes: OUP.

Moyles, J. (1994) *The Excellence of Play*. Milton Keynes: OUP.

NDA/AAHPERD (1991) 'Early Childhood Creative Arts'. Proceedings of the International Childhood Creative Arts Conference, Reston, USA.

NFER (1987) *Four Year Olds In School: Policy and Practice*. NFER SCDC.

Nielsen, L. (1992) *Space and Self*. Copenhagen: Sikon.

North, M. (1972) *Personality Assessment Through Movement*. London: MacDonald & Evans.

Nutbrown, C. (1989) 'Up, Down and Round'. In *Child Education*, May 1989.

Nutbrown, C. (1994) *Threads of Thinking*. London: Paul Chapman Publishing Company.

OFSTED (1993) First Class: The Standards and Quality of Education in Reception Classes. London: HMSO.

Pascal, C. (1990) *Under Fives in Infant Classrooms*. Stoke-on Trent: Trentham Press.

Piaget, J. (1953) *The Origin of Intelligence in the Child*. London: Routledge and Kegan Paul.

Piaget, J. (1962) *Play, Dreams and Imitation in Childhood*. London: Routledge and Kegan Paul.

Piaget, J. (1968) *Six Psychological Studies*. London: University of London Press Ltd.

Piaget, J. and Inhelder, B. (1969) *The Psychology of the Child*. London: Routledge and Kegan Paul.

Pugh, G. and De'Ath, E. (1984) *The Needs of Parents*. London: Macmillan.

Pugh G. (ed.) (1992) *Contemporary Issues in the Early Years*. London: Paul Chapman Publishing Company.

Redfern, H.B. (1973) *Concepts in Modern Educational Dance*. London: Henry Kimpton Publishers.

Richards, C. (1982) *New Directions in Primary Education*. Sussex: The Falmer Press.

Roberts, M. and Tamburrini, J. (eds) (1981) *Child Development 0–5*. Edinburgh: Holmes McDougall.

Rose, C.J. (1978) *Action Profiling; Movement Awareness for Better Management*. London: MacDonald & Evans.

Schaffer, H.R. (1971) *The Growth of Sociability*. London: Penguin.

Schaffer, H.R. (ed.) (1977) *Studies in Mother-Infant Interaction*. London: Academic Press.

# INDEX

Schmidt, R. (1992) *Motor Learning and Performance Instructor's Guide.* Leeds: Human Kinetics Publishers (Europe) Ltd.

Singer, G. and Singer J. (1990) *The House of Make Believe.* London: Harvard University Press.

Shreeves, R. (1990) *Children Dancing.* London: Ward Lock Educational.

Smith-Autard, J.M. (1992) *Dance Composition: a practical guide for teachers.* London: A & C Black Ltd.

Stewart, D. (1990) *The Right To Movement.* London: The Falmer Press.

Stinson, S. (1988) *Dance for Young Children: Finding the Magic in Movement.* Reston, USA: The American Alliance for Health, Physical Education, Recreation and Dance.

Stinson, S. (ed.) *Proceedings of the 1991 Conference of Dance and the Child International.* Salt Lake City: University of Utah.

Sutherland, P. (1992) *Cognitive Development Today: Piaget and His Critics.* London: Paul Chapman Publishing Company.

Swanwick, K. (1983) 'The Arts in Education: Dreaming or Awake? A Special Professorial Lecture'. Institute of Education, London.

Thomas, B. (1993) *Psychology, Child Development and Learning.* London: Royal Academy of Dancing.

Thomas, J., Lee, A., Thomas, K. (1988) *Physical Education for Children: Concepts into Practice.* Illinois: Human Kinetic Books.

Vygotsky, L.S. (1978) *Mind In Society: The Development of Higher Psychological Processes.* London: Harvard University Press.

Wetton, P. (1988) *Physical Education in the Nursery and Infant School.* London: Croom Helm.

Whalley, M. (1994) *Learning to Be Strong: Setting Up a Neighbourhood Service for Under Fives and Their Families.* London: Hodder & Stoughton.

Whitehead, M. (1990) *Language and Literacy in the Early Years,* London: Paul Chapman Publishing Company.

Williams, A. (ed.) (1989) *Issues in Physical Education for the Primary Years.* Lewes: The Falmer Press.

Williams, G. (1988) 'An Attempt to Define Criteria for the Effective Teaching of Dance in the Primary School'. Unpublished MA (Education Studies) thesis. University of Surrey.

Willig, J. (1990) *Children's Concepts and the Primary Curriculum.* London: Paul Chapman Publishing Ltd.

Zaichkowsky, L. D., Zaichkowsky, L. B. and Martinek, T. J. (1980) *The Child and Physical Activity.* St Louis: Mosby.